Through the Interface: A Human Activity Approach to User Interface Design

Susanne Bødker

Computer Science Department
Aarhus University, Denmark

LEA LAWRENCE ERLBAUM ASSOCIATES, PUBLISHERS

1991   Hillsdale, New Jersey   Hove and London

Lawrence Erlbaum Associates, Inc., Publishers
365 Broadway
Hillsdale, New Jersey 07642

Library of Congress Cataloging-in-Publication Data

Bødker, Susanne.
  Through the interface : a human activity approach to user
interface design / Susanne Bødker.
    p. cm.
  Includes bibliographical references and indexes.
  ISBN 0-8058-0570-2. -- ISBN 0-8058-0571-0 (pbk.)
  1. Human-computer interaction. 2. User interfaces (Computer
systems) 3. Systems design. I. Title.
QA76.9.H85B63 1990
005.1--dc20   90-36038
                                                            CIP

Printed in the United States of America

10 9 8 7 6 5 4 3 2 1

Contents

Preface

This book is a slightly revised version of my Ph.D. dissertation from 1987 and the text in most parts stands as it did then. When I started to write this, a number of contributions to a new tradition of understanding human beings and their relation to computer applications had just started to appear.[1] These contributions had not yet made any real impacts on the area of human–computer interaction (HCI). Recently, this HCI community has started to discuss other ways. Norman's example-driven analysis of everyday artifacts, Carroll's and his group's discussions about ecological research, and, not least, Whiteside's work about contextualization are some examples[2]. However, these discussions are still rather premature and often without theoretical foundation.[3]

To my mind, the framework that I present here gives a theoretical foundation for studying the relation between human beings and their computer applications in specific work situations, and I have found it challenging to spread this framework to a wider audience also in America.

I am grateful to all the people who have helped me disseminate this information.

Susanne Bødker

Århus, Denmark, February 1990

---

[1] Suchman, L. (1987). *Plans and situated actions: The problem of human–machine communication.* Cambridge: Cambridge University Press; Winograd, T., & Flores C. F. (1986). *Understanding computers and cognition: A new foundation for design.* Norwood, NJ: Ablex.

[2] Norman, D. (1988). *The psychology of everyday things.* New York: Basic. Carroll, J. & Campbell, R. (1989) Artifacts as Psychological Theories: the case of human–computer interaction. (IBM RC 13454 (# 60225)), Yorktown Heights: IBM, Carroll, J. (Ed.) (1987). *Interfacing thought, cognitive aspects of human–computer interaction.* Cambridge, MA: MIT Press Carroll, J. (1989a). *Evaluation, description, and invention: Paradigms for human–computer interaction* (RC 13926 [#62583]). Yorktown Heights, N.Y.: IBM, Carroll, J. (1989b). Taking artifacts seriously. In S. Maass & H. Oberquelle (Eds.), *Software ergonomie '89* (pp. 36–50). Stuttgart: Tentner. Whiteside, J., & Wixon, D. (1987). Discussion: Improving human–computer interaction–A quest for cognitive science. In J. Carroll, 1987, op. cit. (pp. 353-365).

[3] Bannon, L., & Bødker, S. (in press). Beyond the interface: Encountering artifacts in use. In J. Carroll. (Ed.), *Designing interaction: Psychological theory at the human–computer interface* (publication expected 1990).

Chapter 1

Introduction

> Design is where the action is, not evaluation.
> (Newell & Card)[1]

This book is situated in a field of tension between research traditions that historically have their roots far from each other–in psychology, in computer science, and elsewhere–but that at this point in time are dealing with the same issue: *design of user interfaces*.

I have chosen the title, *Through the interface–A human activity approach to user interface design* to indicate that the book deals with user interfaces and their design from a theoretical perspective that focuses on human work activity and on use of computer applications in human work activity. "Through the interface" tells us that a computer application, from the user's perspective, is not something that the user operates *on* but something that the user operates *through* on other objects or subjects. In this book, the user interface is seen as the parts of software and hardware that support this effect. For example, when I use a text editor to write a document, the user interface supports my work on the form and content of the document, and if the user interface is a good one, I am able to forget that I actually work with a computer between the document and myself.

The traditions

I base myself on the research tradition that has often been called the Aarhus-Oslo school. Its field has been systems development in its broadest sense: analysis and design of computer-based systems and their surrounding organizations as well as the study of impacts of such systems on labor.[2] The

1

background of this school has been to hold a critical attitude toward traditional phase-oriented systems development methods,[3] which have in turn mainly dealt with the development of large batch-oriented computer systems[4] from a management perspective.

However, the character of computer applications is changing of late. There is a shift from large mainframe computers to personal workstations; from data entry and number crunching to interactive, graphics-oriented applications that are no longer solely administrative. Technology provides new possibilities. The data/information-processing paradigm that has been central to our conception of computer applications, is breaking down in more and more situations in which we are dealing with new types of applications. Furthermore, users demand constructive influence in more and more cases, not just a veto against management's suggestions. Management, too, has its reasons to involve users in design.[5]

These changes pose new challenges to our tradition; we need to deal with new kinds of technology: new types of computer applications, new aspects of the applications, and new methods of design. Subsequently, one area of concern is design of user interfaces.

Theoretically, this topic has been dealt with primarily by traditions rooted in psychology: Prototypical examples can be found in the proceedings from the CHI conferences.[6] We can identify at least three different approaches within the tradition: the British human factors tradition, which insists on being an analytic, psychological discipline;[7] the Card–Moran–Newell school[8] which was the first to go directly into design considerations; and for example D. Norman and his group at the University of California at San Diego,[9] the contribution of which can be seen as a new path in psychologists' way of viewing design of user interfaces, a path that is breaking with the cognitive science tradition.

The tradition has been to analyze the users of different computer applications and their reactions toward different user interfaces, for example the difference between keyboard commands and menus for text editors. It has moved from a point where measurement of key stroke speed and the like was the main issue to more advanced analysis of use situations based on theory from cognitive psychology. Some of the promoters of this tradition[10] have come to the conclusion that the field is presently at a point where there is a need for a shift from a quantitative analysis approach to a qualitative design approach: *Design is where the action is in the user interface*. The cognitive science tradition is analyzed in this book in the quest for a renewed understanding of user interfaces and their design.

Perspective

My main focus is computer support for purposeful human work, thus I don't deal with games, casual use of automated bank tellers, and so on. The reasons for this choice can be found in how I came to write my dissertation and in the theory that I have chosen to deal with. Both my empirical experiences and the theoretical framework tells us that what an experienced user does in her daily work is very different from what a casual user of an automated bank teller does. This difference gives rise to a variety of user interfaces. For example, let us consider one aspect of bank tellers: In the use of an automated bank teller, robustness and security is important, and the designers may choose to have push buttons for six or eight different amounts of money that the consumers can withdraw. However, this type of solution would be much too inflexible for the professional banker. But it is no problem to train her, as a regular user, to handle decimal points and large amounts of codes.

When writing or reading a book like this, we face the problem that we cannot learn what we do not already know. Writings are not representations or explanations of the world, they are intended to trigger some awareness by the reader toward his or her own experiences. The challenge is for the writer to trigger the "right" awareness. What we practically understand or know is more important than, and precedes, a theoretical understanding, no matter what domain we talk about: research, design, or typography. This means that any concept arises from, and exists in close connection with, the material world. In most cases, we cannot give complete definitions of concepts but instead point out certain rules and prototypical cases. Through new theories and frameworks, we can create new distinctions in our knowledge of and actions in the material world; but only through the readers' own practical experiences can their value be tested.

It is a basic idea of this book that, for epistemological reasons, participation is needed to improve quality of the design process as well as of the computer application, especially when it comes to the user interface. I have chosen *not* to focus on the more political aspects of user participation in design, for example questions of resources and power. In keeping with my tradition and empirical background, however, I advocate a democratization of design. Participation in design is not the whole of democratic design, only a possible step toward it; trade union investigations, technology agreements, and various negotiation systems are part of the mechanisms needed to move toward democracy.[11] In line with this we must see design as an activity that is a process of negotiation between different groups with conflicting interests and with different resources and power to pursue their goals.

The approach taken

I present here an approach to understanding user interfaces and their design. The idea is to develop the human activity theory that deals with purposeful human work in two areas: one that focuses on computer applications, especially user interfaces, and one that deals with the design of such. What we achieve is not a new theory but a refinement and enrichment of an existing one. But by shifting the focus from human activity to the computer application and its role, we move from a psychological domain to a computer science domain in which we make use of a psychological theory.

The approach presents a point of reference to which actual design processes can be compared. It creates possibilities of seeing some things at the same time as it creates blindness toward others.[12] In this way, the approach is, of course, like all approaches, normative.[13] The actual choice of using the term *design* and not the more common term *development* is an example of this: By using *design* I mean to stress the similarities of the computer expert's trade to other kinds of design, such as architecture, with the former carrying norms such as quality just like these other professions do. At the same time, to choose not to use the term *development* has meant less direct focus on the role that design of computer applications plays in the organizational development process.

Domain and purpose

In design, the user interface is one aspect of the future computer application; the user interface is an object for design. In use, however, the user interface determines how the computer application appears to its user. To understand the user interface we must study the **use** relation between the human and the computer application. The study of this relation has been an issue for psychology, anthropology, and philosophy.

Cognitive science has combined computer science with one school of cognitive psychology. This school believes that a good user interface represents/is based on a model of the user, and even that the user and the computer are structurally alike. Other, more technical definitions[14] see the user interface only from a programmer's perspective, as technical components.

In this book, I explore the possibilities of *offering a new conception of user interfaces*. Toward that end, I present a framework that builds upon the anthropological/psychological theory of Leontjew, whose work offers valuable explanations by its quite operational and detailed explanation of what human beings do when they operate artifacts.[15] Dealing with human work activity means dealing with what is specifically human, compared to objects or animals, especially the ability to design artifacts with the future use activity in mind. Animals may apply sticks and the like as artifacts with specific purposes in specific situations, but only human beings conduct design, imagining the future use of the artifact. Human beings do not conduct design as a well-planned process where we first determine the goals and then the acts. Rather we enter into design as a process where we change our actions as we interact with the material world.

Design of computer applications, seen *not* as a rationalistic and well-planned process but as a process characterized by arationality and action in situations, has been the issue for many authors recently. Winograd and Flores, among others,[16] argued that we need a different theoretical foundation for design. Their suggestions are all based on a combination of several different philosophers. In my discussions of these theories,[17] the challenge arose to investigate how far I could get along the same lines by *trying out the Soviet psychology* as presented by Leontjew and his followers, while directing special attention toward the user interface.

Because a practical understanding is needed to make use of our theoretical understanding, new suggestions for design methods and for user interfaces must follow such new theoretical considerations. Furthermore, new design methods and new user interfaces must be rooted in the specific design situation, which in turn is directed toward the future use situations. This means that I could not expect to give new general guidelines for user interfaces and their design, nor could I sit down at my desk and construct examples, without actually trying out the theory in practical design situations. However, it was not possible within the time frame of my dissertation to supplement the theory with practical experiments. Instead, I discuss here examples from my earlier empirical research within the theoretical frames. In particular, it is an aim of this book to elaborate on the design ideas of the Utopia project, the so-called tools approach[18]–*How can we explain the tools approach and which methods can we develop as part of it?* Through my choice of perspectives I have delimited my object area: computer support for purposeful human work. My goal is not to provide a new method that covers user interface design in all kinds of cases but rather to demonstrate that user interface design under certain conditions can be conducted with success in a specific way. I offer an explanation, and a vocabulary. The readers can use these in their own conception to change their practice. If I am successful, they will understand something new about design, realize new needs, see new goals, and perhaps try out new design methods.

It is not my intention to discuss how such conditions can be achieved. For detailed discussions of the practical constraints of design, the reader is referred to the MARS project.[19] The political constraints have been discussed by Ehn and Kyng, among others.[20] I argue that there are strong epistemological reasons for user participation in user interface design. For democratic reasons, such participation must be followed by resources for unions to support the users.[21] I assume that the needed changes for the less powerful parties–the users and their organizations–can be brought about. How this can be done is only touched on marginally.

My intended audience is those who otherwise read journals and textbooks about human–computer interaction and design of user interfaces. I imagine that the reader is a researcher, teacher, or advanced student in this area or perhaps a person responsible for introducing new ideas or design methods in an industrial organization. My aim has not been to write an introductory textbook.

Personal background

As a student, I favored two subjects, systems development and computer graphics which at the time seemed very distinct. My master thesis work[22] revealed to me, both practically and theoretically, that to write computer programs and to describe human work are two different things, and that formal descriptions are perhaps not the solution in the latter case. However, I moved to more practically oriented surroundings, Xerox PARC, where I worked with computer workstations and programming environments. Moreover, I started to investigate why programming environments had come into being and how they were applied by the users in their design work.

After my return to Denmark, many of my former interests and experiences were united in the UTOPIA project in design with users of graphics oriented applications based on modern computer workstations. The last few years I spent reflecting theoretically on the UTOPIA project: about design together with some former project members and about human–computer interaction with others.[23] Furthermore, I tried to transfer some of the design methods of the project to another domain: offices at Aarhus Polytechnics.

Empirical projects

The book is based on the cases mentioned: the Xerox PARC case, the UTOPIA project, and the Aarhus Polytechnics project. They represent design of user interfaces together with users. The design situations as such are presented in detail in Chapter 3, together with the background and setting of the projects. The UTOPIA project is my main empirical case. It was followed by a smaller project, the Aarhus Polytechnics project which was intended to supplement some of the ideas of UTOPIA in a different domain. Chronologically, my third case, Xerox PARC preceded the two other, and my work there did not aim to gain experience with user interface design. I did, however, gain some experiences relevant for this book.

The UTOPIA project

UTOPIA[24] was a Scandinavian research project on trade union based development of and training in computer technology and work organization, especially text and image processing in the graphic industries.[25] The overall goal of the project was to contribute to the development of powerful skill-enhancing tools for graphic workers, that is the project stressed the development of technology, human qualifications, and education. Quality of work and product was very important. Graphics workers and computer and social researchers worked together on the project, which was carried out at the Swedish Center for Working Life, Stockholm; the Royal Institute of Technology, Stockholm; and the University of Aarhus. The project began in 1981 and went on for 4 years.[26]

The aims were to change the trade unions' range of possible actions at the local level. As an alternative to defending the status quo, the idea was to develop an offensive strategy, by providing and applying technology to improve the quality of work and the products.[27] This technology would be dynamically changeable at individual workplaces as the employees developed their competence. The project also aimed at producing an example that demonstrated that union development of technology was a feasible strategy under certain favorable conditions. It was hoped that the project could inspire the development of strategies on technology policy in different application domains where, for example, the economic, technical, or union conditions were different.

In its first phase, the UTOPIA project investigated existing technology, practice, and training in the graphic industries, as well as the prerequisites for developing alternatives. A major aspect in this phase was the mutual learning process, in which the participants, graphics workers and computer and social researchers, established a common knowledge platform for future work.[28] The project was approached by the publisher and computer supplier Liber, who wished to cooperate under the company's development project TIPS (Text and Image Processing System). Thus, the project came to focus on page makeup and image processing for newspapers, and the next year it concentrated on requirement specification. This called for the development of design methods with which researchers and graphics workers could formulate the requirements together. The project established a technology laboratory[29] with development tools to simulate different kinds of page makeup, image processing, and the surrounding organization. Thus it became possible for the graphics workers to develop requirements and wishes on a concrete level by actually carrying out the page makeup and image processing on simulation equipment. In this laboratory, part of the work aimed at studying and developing user interfaces. This work is the focus for my discussion of the project in the following chapters.

The next step was professional education. Of the more than 20 reports produced in the project, the majority were written for the professional education of the graphics workers.

The cooperation with Liber/TIPS also included an evaluation of the TIPS system and development of work organization in connection with the first pilot installation. However, due to various conflicts between the involved parties, the original objective of active participation in an organizational experiment where graphics workers and journalists could seek new ways together could not be realized. The project has instead followed and evaluated how the technology is used at the pilot plant.[30]

The Aarhus Polytechnics project

The Aarhus School of Polytechnics is the public school for crafts in the Aarhus area. The school is responsible for education and training in such areas as plumbing, metal work, carpentry, printing, and hairdressing. Its administrative activities are partly centralized and partly decentralized being distributed at a number of different locations in the area. These duties include budgets and other financial issues; management of buildings and other facilities; including construction work; registration of students; salaries and other staff administration; supplies, and secretarial work. In this administration a large office automation project was in place, the purpose of which was to create an integrated office automation system that allows for a more efficient administration of the school. The office administration system should be financed not by laying off employees, but by allowing more efficient use of such resources as classrooms and heating.

The project was initiated by management of the school. According to the technology agreement, the project was managed by a technology committee with representation by management and employees. The general objective was that the employees should, in project groups, take part in designing the computer applications that they were to use themselves. The school hired a number of consultants to work with the employees in the design work. The

actual realization of the computer applications was to be carried out by a
computer manufacturer on the basis of the specifications and prototypes
created jointly by the users and the consultants. This case deals with one of
these project groups, computer support for filing. The purpose of the group
was to find out how the file of the school could be reorganized to be more
efficient, eventually by means of a computer application.[31]

The file of all incoming and out-going documents represents the history or
memory of the organization. The retrieval process was, with the chosen
structure of the file, rather cumbersome. The filing office works as a service
function for the caseworkers in the administration, who acquire documents on
specific issues. The project group consisted of the women working in the
filing office, representatives of the caseworkers who were the users of the
file, and consultants with expertise in organizational issues as well as
computers. Two researchers took part with the purpose of trying out design
methods, primarily for user interface design.

The project group worked with three different types of methods: scenarios
to sketch different early alternatives (i. e., different main directions in the
design) simple paper mock-ups of screen images, and prototypes running on
the type of computer equipment that was common in the organization. These
prototypes were based on a fourth generation language.[32] I discuss these
methods throughout the following chapters.

The Smalltalk case

In the early 1970's the Xerox Palo Alto Research Center Learning
Research Group began work on a vision of the ways different people
might effectively and joyfully use computing power. In 1981 the name of
the group was changed to the Software Concepts Group or SCG. The goal
of SCG is to create a powerful information system, one in which the user
can store, access and manipulate information so that the system can grow
as the user's ideas grow. Both the number and kinds of system
components should grow in proportion to the growth of the user's
awareness of how to effectively use the system.[33]

SCG has been concentrating on two areas of research: a programming
language and a user interface, which supports the user in her programming
effort. The programming language and system is called Smalltalk-80, which
is an object-oriented language, based on a small number of concepts. The
whole system is, in principle, written in the Smalltalk language itself, and as
such is accessible to the user.

Smalltalk is a graphical, interactive programming environment. As
suggested by the personal computing vision, Smalltalk is designed so that

every component in the system that is accessible to the user can be presented in a meaningful way for observation and manipulation. The user interface issues in Smalltalk revolve around the attempt to create a visual language for each object. The preferred hardware system for Smalltalk includes a high-resolution graphical display screen and a pointing device such as a graphical pen or a mouse. With these devices, the user can select information viewed on the screen and invoke messages in order to interact with that information.[34]

In 1982–83 I spent 8 months with the SCG, sharing the daily life and work of the group. During that period I participated in a couple of the projects in the group, and I conducted interviews with the group members concerning their practice and conception of the Smalltalk-80 language and environment. What I have chosen to call the Smalltalk case is an extraction of the various experiences concerning design of the user interface that I gained from this stay. These experiences illustrate what it means for design of user interfaces to be appropriate for the users: Users and designers are the same group of people, that is we can take the user interface of the Smalltalk-80 system as an expression of what the users need. We can furthermore see the Smalltalk-80 environment as expressing the designers' needs.

The group had access to the most advanced computer technology, to very competent computer people, and the researchers had, to a large extent, the freedom and resources to pursue their own ideas, as individuals and as a group. Although management at times intervened in the design process, this could be seen as quite an ideal situation.

Theoretical background

Theoretically, this book begins and ends in computer science. My intention is to facilitate better user interface design, which means to begin and end with what computers and computer applications are, and how they can be constructed to function as efficiently as possible. To assess efficiency, however, we need a different kind of methods than those needed to assess, for instance, the efficiency of algorithms. In the evolution of computer science, the theory of algorithms and their efficiency has developed out of mathematics. To deal with the "efficiency" of the user interface we need not only to deal with the computer but with the interplay between human beings and computers. Computer science is not capable of offering its own explanation of this relation. Just as computer science earlier borrowed theory from mathematics, language theory,[35] and so forth, we need to look for sciences that can help us in our current aims. Other fields of computer science, especially expert systems, are presently in a similar situation.

Within the area of user interface design, cognitive science is one way of bringing in another science. I discuss the practical applicability of these results. The philosophical impacts are discussed by, for example Winograd and Flores, Suchman, and Dreyfus and Dreyfus.[36] Their critique is part of a new and evolving theoretical approach, one that considers human activity, including design or use of computer applications, not as primarily characterized by rationality, planning, and reflection, but by practice and our ability to act in situations, which are more or less familiar to us, where reflection is something secondary or post factum. The thoughts of a number of otherwise different philosophers are used in these approaches: Winograd and Flores, and others with them, have used the ideas of Heidegger and Gadamer in their work. The thoughts of Wittgenstein have been used by Ehn, Lundequist, Göranzon, and others,[37] and all of these have inspired me in my work. The courses taught by, and my discussions with, Pelle Ehn and Morten Kyng have opened my eyes for these ideas, as well as for the thoughts of Polanyi,[38] and the Soviet psychology,[39] which I came to focus on. Whereas Heidegger and Wittgenstein produced their work as general philosophy, the aims of Winograd and Flores, Suchman, Dreyfus and Dreyfus, Ehn, Göranzon, and others were to create a new foundation for design of computer applications and for understanding the role of computers in the life of human beings, in general or in specific human activities, such as work.

I do not go into long discussions about the similarities and differences among these schools of thought. The interested reader will find this discussed by Ehn.[40] Rather, I repeat one reason and state another for choosing to focus on the Soviet psychology. First, although all the theories share the fundamental idea that practice is the basis for the being and doing of human beings, they differ in the way they consider language: To Winograd and Flores, all activity is primarily communication. The lack of consideration for the physical activity underlying the activity results in a view of practice as something that exists for each individual human being. As for the ideas of Dreyfus and Dreyfus,[41] the problem is that they primarily discuss the learning and competence of the individual; not that competence is bound to the material conditions, that artifacts used in some activity, as well as the materials used, are carrying a certain practice, and that competence is social. The work of Leontjew[42] has the advantage of considering practice both in relation to the material conditions shared by a group of human beings and to the way this is reflected in the consciousness of the individual. Second the approach taken by, for example, Winograd and Flores is to bring together pieces of different theories from different traditions. With this comes the problem of convincing the reader as well as oneself that the theories can be applied together, that they do not build on conflicting assumptions, and so on. I try to avoid this by starting from within one school of thought. Soviet psychology seemed to offer a better chance for this than the rest.

It is the fundamental idea of Soviet psychology as presented by Leontjew and others to get to an understanding of society or culture on the one hand, personality on the other, and primarily of the connection between the two. To do this they unite aspects of sociology, historical materialism, and psychology into a theory that takes its starting point in human activity as the basic component in purposeful human work. It is not my intention to go into abstract and philosophical discussions about this theory, but, inspired by Danish psychologists,[43] I present a concrete framework about computer applications, their role in human work activity, and the impacts of this for design. By this approach I start from a theory about human beings and the role of computer applications in work and apply this theory to get to a framework by which we can deal with computer application and the design of such. My special concern is for the user interface, because, as we see, this is essential for how the computer application appears to its user in use.

Design of user interface is a topic that relates to a number of disciplines in computer science. We can see the framework that I present in this book as one way of extending our theoretical foundation within the areas of human–computer interaction and design of user interfaces. The value of this extension is ultimately tested through the explanations that is offered in the book, of known phenomena, and when my suggestions for design of user interfaces have been tried out in practical design. The latter is not part of the dissertation work.

Structure of the book

I have presented the theoretical and the empirical backgrounds separately, and I have stressed the fact that it was the empirical background that generated the need for a new theory. However, the dialectics between the empirical and the theoretical results are what really matters. Although the structure of this report is determined by theory, I use empirical examples throughout the report to explain the theory and I give concrete examples of what the new theory means at the empirical level. Furthermore, it is important to look back at traditional theoretical frameworks and methods for design of user interfaces to see how they can be viewed in light of our new theory. Hopefully, this can help explain both the discrepancy between design practice and traditional methods, and the need for a changed practice.

Naturally, the subject is centered around the computer applications or **computer-based artifact**. The artifacts are employed by users in use activities to create some product or achieve some goal. The use activity and the intended product is, on the one hand, part of determining how the artifact can be employed. On the other, the actual construction of the artifact is part of determining which use situations and products can be created. Similar dialectic relations exist between the design activity and the computer-based artifact, between the design situation and the design methods that can be employed, and so on. I have chosen to focus on some of these relations in the structure of the report. In Chapter 2, I present the overall theoretical framework of the book. The framework is illustrated by examples from the empirical studies. In Chapter 3, a number of design activities are presented. They present the empirical background and function as examples in the following chapters. From the theoretical framework of Chapter 2, in Chapter 4 I elaborate on the parts concerning the user interface to get to a more detailed understanding of the user interface and its relations to the design and the use situations. Whereas Chapter 4 emphasizes the user interface, Chapter 5 focuses on design of user interfaces. I discuss various design methods and their way of handling the user interface design. Furthermore, I discuss the applicability of different kinds of design techniques to improve the user interface design. In Chapter 6, I use the conclusions of the previous chapters to provide a number of concrete recommendations for designers of user interfaces. I hope that these recommendations, as well as the rest of the book, can be used to give designers inspiration to change their practice.

This book by no means looks at design methods as something that can be followed like a computer executing a program. Rather, it views design methods as something that can point at various ways of changing design practice in specific situations. There are many limits to the kinds of design activities dealt with in the book and I do not claim that the experiences are generally transferable outside the discussed types of design situations. I think, however, that the ideas can be used for designers within other and perhaps more traditional application domains; by presenting alternatives, the book allows designers to reflect on their own practice and eventually perhaps change it. The ideas, hopefully, can be used by researchers and students who want to deal with user interfaces, either on a practical or on a more theoretical level. On the practical level I think that the book offers explanations as to why the human–computer interaction functions the way it does in a number of situations, as well as offers valuable recommendations for design.

---

[1]Newell, A. & Card, S. (1985). The prospects for psychological science in human–computer interaction, *Human Computer Interaction, 1*, p. 214.

2 A good survey of this tradition can be found in Bjerknes, G., Ehn, P., & Kyng, M., (Eds.) (1987) *Computers and democracy: A Scandinavian challenge.* Aldershot, UK: Avebury.

3 See, for example, SIS handbok 113. (1973). *Riktslinjer för administrativ systemutveckling* [Guidelines for administrative systems development]. Stockholm: SIS.

4 See, for example the analysis of graphical systems description tools in Bødker, S., & Hammerskov, J. (1982). *Grafisk systembeskrivelse* [Graphical systems description] (DAIMI IR-33, IR-34, and IR-35). Århus: University of Aarhus.

5 Historically, we have seen different trends in management's attempts and reasons to involve users: from sociotechnical satisfaction and autonomous groups, via technology agreements with user participation in the control of traditional phase-oriented systems development projects, to active user involvement in both project groups and project management (see Ehn, P., & Kyng, M. (1987). The collective resource approach to systems design. In G. Bjerknes et al. (pp. 17–58). op. cit. [note 2]). Many examples of this type of management strategy can be found in the public sector in Scandinavia today. I examine one of these cases in this book.

6 Janda, A. (Ed.) (1983). *Human factors in computing systems.* Proceedings, ACM.

7 See, for example, Hammond, N., Helms Jørgensen, A., Maclean, A., Barnard, P., & Long, J. (1983). Design practice and interface usability: Evidence from interviews with designers. In Janda, (pp. 40–44), ibid.

8 See Card, S., Moran, T., & Newell, A. (1983). *The psychology of human–computer interaction.* Hillsdale, NJ: Lawrence Erlbaum Associates.

9 See Norman, D. A., & Draper, S. W. (Eds.) (1986). *User–centered system design.* Hillsdale, NJ: Lawrence Erlbaum Associates.

10 Card et al., op. cit. (note 8).

11 Ehn & Kyng, op. cit. (note 5).

12 Winograd, T., & Flores C. F. (1986). *Understanding computers and cognition: A new foundation for design.* Norwood, NJ: Ablex.

13 Things can be normative in different ways, and especially for design we can make an important distinction between the way that certain design methods are normative in stating how design should be conducted and the way, as described in the text, that frameworks are normative in creating certain distinctions in our conception of a phenomenon.

14 Newman, W. M., & Sproull, R. F. (1979). *Principles of interactive computer graphics* (2nd ed.). Tokyo: McGraw-Hill or Foley, J. D., & van Dam, A. (1982). *Fundamentals of interactive computer graphics.* Reading, MA: Addison-Wesley.

[15] A detailed discussion of the relation between the theories can be found in Ehn, P. (1988). *Work-oriented design of computer artifacts*. Falköping, Sweden: Arbetslivscentrum/Almqvist & Wiksell International.

[16] Winograd & Flores, op. cit. (note 12), Ehn, op. cit. (note 15), Andersen, N. E., Kensing, F., Lassen, M., Lundin, J., Mathiassen, L., Munk-Madsen, A., & Sørgaard, P. (1990). *Professional system development: Experience, ideas, and action*. Englewood Cliffs, NJ: Prentice Hall and Suchman, L. (1987). *Plans and situated actions: The problem of human–machine communication*. Cambridge: Cambridge University Press.

17 Many of these discussions took place during two graduate courses taught by Pelle Ehn and Morten Kyng at DAIMI: "The Computer as a Tool" and "Design and Cognition". Also a study group with researchers from the Institutes of Psychology and of Information Science and a talk with Terry Winograd have been important.

[18] Ehn, P., & Kyng, M. (1984). A tool perspective on design of interactive computer support for skilled workers. In M. Sääksjärvi (Ed.), *Proceedings from the Seventh Scandinavian Research Seminar on Systemeering* (pp. 211–242). Helsinki: Helsinki Business School.

19 Andersen et al., op. cit. (note 16).

[20] Ehn & Kyng, 1987, op. cit. (note 5).

[21] See for example, Ehn & Kyng's (ibid.) discussion of union investigatory work.

[22] Bødker & Hammerskov, op. cit. (note 4).

23 Many former project members participated in the Dialog project at the Royal Institute of Technology in Stockholm, a project on human–computer interaction for graphic work. I had the honor of being a friend of the project, i. e., I was invited to several of the project's seminars. Along with John Kammersgaard, I did both theoretical and practical follow-up of the ideas from the UTOPIA project (Bødker, S., & Kammersgaard, J. (1984). *Interaktionsbegreber* [Interaction concepts]. Unpublished manuscript).

[24] This presentation is based on Bødker, S., Ehn, P., Kammersgaard, J., Kyng, M., & Sundblad, Y. (1987). A Utopian experience. In Bjerknes et al., (pp. 251–278), op cit. (note 2).

[25] In the Scandinavian languages, UTOPIA is an acronym for Training, Technology, and Products from a Quality of Work Perspective.

[26]The strategic background of the UTOPIA project can be found in the UTOPIA research programme from 1980 (Ehn, P., Kyng, M., & Sundblad, Y. (1981). *Training, technology, and product from the quality of work perspective, A Scandinavian research project on union based development of and training in computer technology and work organization, especially text and image processing in the graphic industry* (UTOPIA Report No. 2). Stockholm: Arbetslivscentrum, p. 7.): The

experience gained by organized labor and the research conducted by trade unions during the 1970's into the ability to influence new technology and the organization of work at local level highlighted a number of problems. One fundamental experience gained is that the "degrees of freedom" available to design the content and organization of work which utilizes existing technology is often considerably less than that required to meet trade union's demands. Or expressed another way: Existing production technology more and more often constitutes an insurmountable barrier preventing the realization of trade union demands for the quality of work and a meaningful job.

27 Discussions about the UTOPIA project and its predecessors as union strategy and as research strategy can be found in Ehn & Kyng, op. cit. (note 5).

28 The UTOPIA project was a big and geographically segregated project, and, furthermore, I did not take part in the project until 1983. For that reason I consider myself more of an observer of what happened in the project than one who did the work. On the other hand, it is hard to talk like an outsider, about a project that you took part in. I have chosen to talk about we–we the project, but the reader should know that I often took no part in what we did. I note when this distinction is important.

29 See S. Bødker et al., op. cit. (note 24) or Bødker, S., Ehn, P., Romberger, S., & Sjögren, D. (Eds.) (1985). *Graffiti 7. The UTOPIA project: An alternative in text and images*. Stockholm:Arbetslivcentrum.

30 Bartholdy, M., Nordquist, C., & Romberger, S. (1987). *Studie av DATORSTÖDD BILD-BEHANDLING på Aftonbladet* [A study of computer-supported image processing at Aftonbladet] (UTOPIA Report No. 21). Stockholm: Arbetslivscentrum.

31 For a more detailed discussion of the project and the specific case, see Kristensen, B. H., Bollesen, N., & Sørensen, O. L. (1986). *Retningslinier for valg af faglige strategier på kontorområdet–et case studie over Århus tekniske Skoles kontorautomatiseringsprojekt* [Guidelines for trade union strategies in the office area: A case study of the office automation project of the Aarhus School of Polytechnics]. Unpublished master's thesis, Department of Computer Science, University of Aarhus.

32 Although the work in the project group took place during working hours the participants still had to do their regular work. No resources were available for hiring extra employees to take over some of the work. This made it hard for the employees to give priority to the project. Management, on the other hand, had different priorities. Because they had more time, management often took the initiative, both when it came to initiating new projects and to making specific design suggestions. Furthermore, the role of the consultants was quite problematic: On the one hand, they were intended to work for the technology committee, meaning that they should act unbiased in the project group. On the other, they were hired by management and management made use of them in other situations. This meant that suggestions from the consultants

were often interpreted as directives from management, and the employees did not have similar possibilities for having their own consultants.

33 Goldberg, A., & Robson, D. (1983). *SMALLTALK-80: The language and its implementation*. Reading, MA: Addison-Wesley.

34 Ibid.

35 For example. N. Chomsky and others who worked on syntactic descriptions of languages, including formal languages.

36 Winograd & Flores, op. cit. (note 12), Suchman op. cit. (note 16), and Dreyfus, H., & Dreyfus, S. (1986). *Mind over machine: The power of human intuition and expertise in the era of the computer*. Glasgow: Basil Blackwell.

37 Wittgenstein, L. (1953). *Philosophical investigations*. Oxford: Oxford University Press, Ehn, op. cit. (note 15), Lundequist, J. (1982). *Norm och modell* [Norm and model]. Unpublished doctoral dissertation, The Royal Institute of Technology, Stockholm, and Göranzon, B. (Ed.) (1984). *Datautvecklingens filosofi* [The philosophy of computer development]. Malmö, Sweden: Carlsson & Jönsson.

38 Polanyi, M. (1967). *Personal knowledge*. London: Routledge & Kegan Paul.

39 Leontjew, A. N. (1981b). *Problems of the development of the mind*. Moscow: Progress, Leontjew, A. N. (1978). *Activity, consciousness, and personality*. Englewood Cliffs, NJ: Prentice-Hall, or Cole, M., & Maltzman, I. (Eds.) (1969). *A handbook of contemporary Soviet psychology*. New York: Basic.

40 Ehn, op. cit. (note 15).

41 Dreyfus& Dreyfus, op. cit. (note 36).

42 Leontjew, 1981, op. cit. (note 39).

43 See for example. Karpatschof, B. (1984). Grænsen for automatisering [The Limit of automation]. *Psyke og Logos, 2*, 201–220.

Chapter 2

Human Activity and Human–Computer Interaction

> It is clear that (and has been widely recognized) that one cannot understand a technology without having a *functional* understanding of how it is used. Furthermore, that understanding must incorporate a *holistic* view of the network of technologies and activities into which it fits, rather than treating the technological devices in isolation. (Winograd & Flores)[1]

Throughout recent years, the use of computers has shifted from calculation or information processing to a wider variety of applications, and the direct contact between the human and the computer becomes more and more advanced. We have moved from a situation where a few computer specialists interacted with computers through punch cards to a situation where computers are operated by office workers, professionals, and craftspeople, as well as by unskilled workers in their work.

Our theoretical conception of what goes on between the human being and the computer when the human uses a computer for a specific task has not followed this rapid development. In this book the aim is to contribute to such a theoretical conception. Taking the words *human–computer communication* or *human–computer interaction* literally means that we consider what goes on between a human being and a computer the same way we consider interpersonal communication. The human being is

18

communicating with something that is, although not human, a communication partner. It becomes the research goal for design of the user interface to exploit the computer's capabilities to act as or instead of a human being in communication situations. In design, this perspective may be useful, but many applications are not of this character: A drawing program like MacPaint,[2] seen as a communication partner, would lead to requirements such as to be able to direct the pen with commands in natural language. There are obvious reasons to doubt that artists or architects think of their real pen as a communication partner and that this type of perspective is reasonable for computer-based pens.

We can also interpret communication or interaction as a human being communicating with other human beings through a computer-based **medium**. We focus on how to mediate the communication between the user and the human at the other end of the medium, whether it is the programmer or the actual partner in communication. It becomes important to understand how human beings act in communication situations and how this must be reflected in the computer medium.[3] But again, can all computer applications be conceived as media? Who is communicating with whom in a drawing program?

Other frameworks focus on the use of computer applications for specific work tasks, comparing this to the use of traditional tools.[4] By applying a tools perspective we focus on the work process and on the human use of tools to process some material into products. The material conditions for the use process become important: The users' competence, reflects the practice of the group of users. The human–computer interaction is seen as part of the actual execution of the work process. However, we can ask whether all computer applications benefit from being perceived as tools. What do we see if we view an electronic mail system as a tool? We see how we can write down a text perhaps, but more important for electronic mail is probably another aspect: that we can communicate with other human beings through the mail system.

No matter which of these approaches to human–computer interaction[5] we choose, we see examples indicating that the perspective is not rich enough to cover all types of well-known applications. Neither an isolated the-user-and-her-tool perspective, nor a pure media or communication perspective seems sufficient for understanding human–computer interaction. We need a framework to deal with both communication and tool use in work situations where computers are involved. This is approached here in the following way: When conducting some work process, you do more than just interact with your computer. You create a product through the tool or you communicate through the medium. You communicate with your work mates, be it to learn about your tools, materials, and products in a problem situation or to coordinate the common effort. Communication does not just take place isolated from the relation with materials and products–linguistic meaning is formed in humans' joint labor activity, to contribute to the overall goal of work. Human–computer interaction is part of the specific work activity in which the computer is applied.

The main purpose of this book is to understand human–computer interaction and the conditions for this, that is the user interface. In the literature, human–computer interaction is often considered either as something that can be considered totally independent of the specific use situation or as something that is specific for the specific user in the specific use situation.[6] The idea here is that on the one hand the human–computer interaction cannot be seen independently of the use situation. Many aspects are important, for example, whether the interaction is part of a communication or a production of some more or less tangible product. On the other hand, we need an understanding of user interfaces that does not just focus on the needs of the individual user in a specific situation. The reason for this is that we need to design computer applications to be used by more than one user; a theory that aims only at design for specific individuals seems elitist and has hardly any practical applicability.

In this chapter, the goal is to reach further than just an analytic framework by which human–computer interaction can be conceived in specific use situations, and further than a design strategy for user interface design. The idea is to elaborate on *a theory about human–computer interaction as part of a theory of human work.* The approach focuses on the use of computer-based artifacts[7] in human work activity and, thus, on the role of the user interface and of human–computer interaction in a specific work activity. Specific for human life, the way it is viewed here, is that human beings, as opposed to animals or things, create artifacts to be applied in a *future* use activity. By choosing this type of approach I concentrate on computer use as it occurs in purposeful work, with a specific organization and division of work, and based on a specific practice of the users.[8]

This presentation is as follows: a general presentation of the human activity theory, a section where I present my elaboration of this theory into a theory about computer-based artifacts, a similar section on design of artifacts, and finally, a summary and discussion of the framework.

Human work activity

In this section I give a short presentation or interpretation of the relevant part of the human activity theory. The presentation is primarily based on the work of Leontjew, [9] Hydén,[10] and Karpatschof.[11] But my thoughts and ideas are also inspired by Wittgenstein,[12] Polanyi,[13] and Winograd and Flores.[14] The purpose of this section is to provide the reader with sufficient background for understanding the following sections in which I use the theory and elaborate on it.[15]

An introductory example

We can look at makeup of newspaper pages.[16] As the basic component, page makeup is conducted by one or more persons, each carrying out their own **individual** page makeup **activity**.

The activity of the individual human being, such as page makeup, is part of the **collective** activity of various groups, for example, the makeup persons at the specific newspaper or the persons handling the front page of a specific newspaper. The individual makeup activity has a goal or we can say that it is directed toward an object: the newspaper page. The individual page makeup activity contributes to the goals of the collective activity, for instance, the activity of the group of persons–reporters, editors, and typographers–handling the front page. This goal could be to promote a certain story, perhaps in turn to make the paper sell better. The makeup person places the story at the top of the front page, uses a certain size of headline, and so on. These things have a meaning to the front page group, but probably also to the readers of the paper.

To organize, coordinate, and control the collective activity, **communication** plays a role. This means that the makeup persons direct some parts of their activity toward other human beings or subjects, for example, the editors or each other. We call this the **communicative side** of human activity, when, for example, the makeup person discusses with the editor how to have the articles fit onto the page. Other parts are directed toward objects, the **instrumental side**: The makeup person handles paper galleys, pictures, and so forth, to actually create the front page.

The makeup person uses **artifacts** in the activity. Both the instrumental and the communicative side can be **mediated** by artifacts. A knife or a pair of scissors mediate the instrumental side, the forming of the newspaper page. Layout sketches, production plans, and so on, mediate the communicative side, the coordination of the production.

We can view the individual human activity as conducted through **actions**, which take place in a unity of time and space **with specific intentions**. Making-up a specific newspaper page may consist of placing an ad in the bottom right-hand corner, fitting in some text between the ad and a picture, and so forth. An action is conducted through one or more **operations**, which are bound to specific material conditions. To place an ad, the makeup person picks up the photo typesetter paper,[17] picks up the knife, cuts off some of the white area around the ad if there is too much white, all without being aware of this. The right operation to be used in a specific situation is **triggered** by the material conditions; it is not chosen consciously by the typographer. When the typographer places an ad, we can say that the actions are what he or she is consciously doing, for example, placing an ad in the bottom right-hand corner, whereas the operations are what he or she does to realize this, for example, hold knife, cut paper, try position on page ground. In addition, what in some situations are actions can in other situations be conducted as operations that are part of other actions: For example, placing a picture can be something that has its own specific purpose, or it can be conducted as as part of placing an article on the page ground.

Through learning, in special learning activities or in daily work activities, people obtain a repertoire of operations to be used in a specific activity. They get to share the **practice** of typographers at the same time as they are part of constituting this practice. Those responsible for page makeup can reflect upon what were formerly operations and try to perform former operations as actions, for example if the editor tells them that the editor is not pleased with the product of the typographer. We call this **conceptualization**. Changing the level of action means changing the object (or subject) of the actions: Instead of working on the article, the makeup person starts to think about headlines, pictures, and the like. Unforeseen changes in the material conditions in the specific page makeup activity may cause conceptualization. We call such situations **breakdowns**.

Situations where the makeup person's knife causes a breakdown could be: while learning to use a new kind of knife; if the knife breaks; if the knife is badly suited for the kind of cutting its user wants to achieve, a switch of knife can be necessary; or a special handling of the knife to achieve the intended result. In such situations, the knife is no longer something that is handled only through operations. Rather, the knife becomes the object for the actions, removing the focus from the real object, the newspaper page.

Summary of the human activity theory

In this section I present the main concepts and ideas of my interpretation of the work of Leontjew and others.[18] **Human work activity** is the basic component of this theory. A human being conducts each concrete **action**, through which any activity is conducted. The concrete actions that a human being conducts contribute to an individual human activity: a process through which the human being produces some kind of relation to the physical and social world around her.

The human being can aim to achieve a goal in the activity, that is aim at solving a task or problem, and she can direct her activity toward some physical object, some material that is to be affected through the activity. We can say that all activity is bound to a **goal** and/or an **object**. What in some situations is an intention of an action may in other situations become an activity with a purpose in itself, and vice versa. Whereas in some situations artists paint a picture to make a living, in other situations they may paint just to make a specific picture.

The characteristics of the goal or object partially determine and structure the activity. If a human being deals with a physical object, the physical structure of the object will delimit which actions to perform, how, and in what sequence. If the task is to collect some information from various physical and human sources, the physical and social structure–where to start, whom to talk with and how, and so forth–will determine the structure.

The production by the human being of her relation to the material world goes on in this way: On the one hand, some need will cause the subject to perform actions, with certain **intentions**, which intervene with the physical and social world, for example, to change a specific object. This intervention is based on a mental reflection of the world, including the specific object. On the other hand, as, say, a physical object is structuring the actions of the human being, the reflection of the object is created and changed through the actions. U. Juul-Jensen says about reflection: ". . . human consciousness is a reflection of the social and material world we live in. This does not mean that consciousness consists of a special kind of images which in some ways resemble the objective world. That consciousness is reflection of the world means that the physiological structures by which it is constituted are products of our activity in this world."[19]

In the human activity, different **means** are employed: cultural techniques, such as ways of structuring the individual actions; artifacts, for example hammers or telephones; and languages. Through these means, the human being mediates her relation with the world.

Human beings always participate in various activities. These collective activities are structured according to a certain order of the society in which they take place. The individual will meet this order through power relations, institutions, and grouping of interest in society, under which the human being lives, at the same time as she can contribute to their change. In most societies, the division of labor has caused a separation of the needs of the individual and the goal of the activity in which she takes part. Furthermore, the needs of the individual as part of different collective activities might differ and even conflict.[20] We can say that the human being has not one need in the concrete activity but a whole cluster, some of which are conflicting.

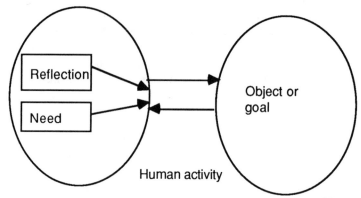

Figure 2.1. Human reflection of the social and material world[21]

In collective activity, language is used to coordinate work. Each individual activity consists of communication with others human beings to organize, coordinate, and control the activity, and of actions directed toward things that serve as objects or artifacts in the material production. We talk about the **communicative** and the **instrumental** side of human activity.

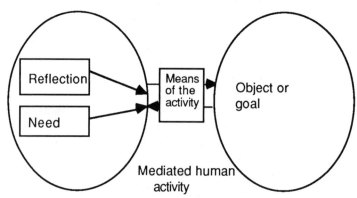

Figure 2.2. The mediated activity

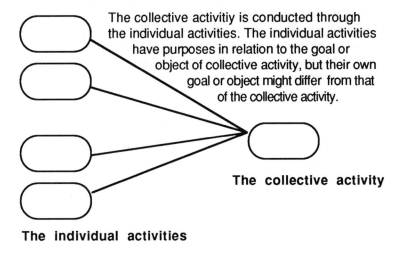

The collective activitiy is conducted through the individual activities. The individual activities have purposes in relation to the goal or object of collective activity, but their own goal or object might differ from that of the collective activity.

The collective activity

The individual activities

Figure 2.3. The outer levels of human activity

We can look at an example about programming. When I[22] use the Smalltalk-80 system to program something like some code to take care of my household finances, my activity is primarily part of financing my household. In my activity, my actions on the budget, and so on, are mediated by the Smalltalk-80 system. My Smalltalk-80 programming, of course, aims at producing an overview of my household finances (the instrumental side), and perhaps I even direct my actions toward the computer application as such (instrumental) in situations where the Smalltalk-80 system becomes the object for my actions. For example, if I open a window that gets placed on top of what I am doing, I need to aim my actions at moving or removing the window. At the same time, I might need the overview to discuss it with my family or my bank (communicative side). And in case of errors in my programs, I might contact somebody who knows more about Smalltalk programming than I do.

Actions

Each individual activity is conducted through **actions**, conducted in a unity of time and space, with specific **intentions** (*what* ought to be done). It is because of the intentional aspects of the actions and activity that we can communicate about the instrumental side of our activity–that our instrumental activity has a meaning to us. These actions are consciously directed toward an object or a subject. Each action that a human being carries out also has **operational** aspects (*how* is it done).

In the activity, the intentions of the actions might not relate directly to the goal or object of the activity. To create statistics about the frequency and habits of Macintosh users, we might interview people, design questionnaires, draw tables, or ask somebody whom to interview.

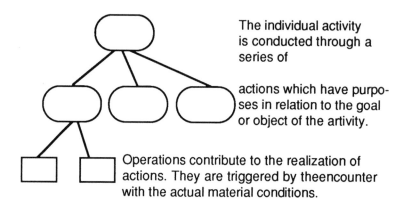

The individual activity is conducted through a series of

actions which have purposes in relation to the goal or object of the artivity.

Operations contribute to the realization of actions. They are triggered by theencounter with the actual material conditions.

Figure 2.4. The individual human activity. Note that this is not a static picture of how a certain activity is (always) conducted, but more like a snapshot of a situation.

In the Smalltalk-80 example, I use the artifacts in my activity: I use the mouse to move the cursor around the display; I press the left button to select items on the screen; I press the middle button to show me a menu of various things to do; I can select a command by moving the cursor to the specific entry in the menu while holding down the middle button; I can activate the program by letting go of the middle button. However, when I program I don't think about pressing and releasing mouse buttons, and so on. These are operations to me. I think about creating an object called household finances, creating a method to show my expenditures. Maybe I remember that I can copy a piece of code from some similar method. I open the browser, find the method I am interested in, and so on. These are the actions that I do, on purpose or intentionally, to fulfill the goals of my activity.

Operations

The operational aspects of actions are implemented through a series of **operations**. Each operation corresponds to the concrete material (physical or social) conditions for implementation of the actions, and it is triggered by the appearance of those specific concrete material conditions. Operations are sensomotor units that a human being performs in a specific situation, without consciousness, to carry out the actions of which the human being is conscious.

Individuals possess a certain **repertoire** of operations. This repertoire is part of the conditions of a specific activity because they form the basis from which operations are triggered by meeting up with concrete material conditions. For each concrete action, the human being is dependent on the triggering of a sequence of operations. If these do not exist, she must consciously carry out different actions. Most likely, she must carry out more detailed actions due to the lack of operations. A simple example is writing a letter with a new word processor–we need not only be conscious of writing the letter but also of turning on the computer, opening the editor, and so forth. Actions can be **operationalized**,[23] that is turned into operations. Operations can be **conceptualized**. Conceptualization means to articulate for oneself what is otherwise self-evident. When we use a new word processor we know, or become conscious of, that we cannot just operate it the way we did with the old one, and we carry out what were formerly operations as actions.

The operations applied in a specific action are not conscious to the human being. But through conceptualization they can be made conscious to us as the actions they once were; we can name a specific sequence of operations and understand and explain reasons for their application at the level that was the level of the former actions. In specific situations, or after carrying out a specific activity, we can ask a person how and why she did what she did.

Conceptualization can take place in **breakdown situations**,[24] situations in which some unarticulated conflict occurs between the assumed conditions for the operations on the one hand, and the actual conditions on the other; between the human reflection of the material conditions, and the actual conditions. Let's assume that we can use the new word processor like the old one, and we start to write a letter. We might succeed with this for a while, but sooner or later something will probably be different and we are forced to see letter writing as something that requires other operations, and thus, other actions. For the purpose of design, it is interesting to focus on the character of the operations and their material conditions: In design we are going to change operations and their conditions for a specific activity, and for that reason we need to focus on both actual operations and conditions, and future changed ones.

However, we cannot ask the person to predict her future operations in a future action. She will not know these until they are done; they are triggered by the material conditions, by the confrontation with the actual nature or culture, not by any quantifiable set of conditions. We say that the operations are usually **nonarticulated**, we are not aware of them, but they can be articulated in after-the-fact reflection or breakdowns.[25] The material conditions are often **nonarticulable**, that is, we cannot articulate which set of material conditions made us use one operation instead of another. This gives an action a certain sense of unpredictability. Even though it is possible to get to know something about which repertoire of operation is possessed by the human being for some purpose, neither the person herself nor any observer can predict which operations come into play in the specific activity of use.

In my programming, I sometimes operate at one level of actions: When I have programmed my "show expenditures" method, I want to try it, and I issue the command "do it". At other times, I operate on other levels. If I want only a part of the method executed, I might choose another strategy: select the program text that I want executed and then issue "do it." Things can happen that bring the former operations into my consciousness, such as if a wrong menu shows up when I want to say "do it". Did I press the wrong mouse button? Or did I select a wrong item before opening the menu? To find out and to have the right thing done, I need to carry out my former operation step-by-step: select the right place, press the left button, move the cursor (and mouse) to do the selection, release the leftmost button when the text has been selected, press the middle button, move the cursor until "do it" is highlighted, release the middle button.

I often found myself in similar situations when I started to use Smalltalk-80: I needed to think consciously about every tiny step, but after some training my focus moved to the programs that I made, I operationalized some of my former actions into operations. In this example, I have actually articulated some of the usually nonarticulated aspects: my operations on the artifact, the Smalltalk-80 system, and on the problem of financing my household. This articulation will, however, not lead to any predictions about what I will do in another, similar activity, because the material conditions might at that time trigger a different combination of operations.

Practice

A group of human beings who conduct a collective activity with a specific object or goal shares a **practice**. The practice of a group arises from, and is carried by, some common goal or object, as well as by the conditions of the collective activity, such as materials and organizational surroundings, and the **means** of the activity. Practice is reflected in the repertoire of operations of the individual member of the group, at the same time as the individual member take part in constituting and producing the practice of the group through her actions and operations.

The means of the activity are important carriers of practice. The **cultural techniques** that are specific ways of doing things, along with spoken language, belong to one category: They can be made explicit through articulation of the nonarticulated, but they are only present in the activity through actions and operations being carried out by persons on physical objects or subjects. Written language and artifacts, which are either **passive** or **active externalized**, can be present as objects independent of the actions of a human being. A passive externalized artifact facilitates a person's implementation of certain operations, whereas an active externalized artifact, besides from facilitating certain operations, also replaces certain former operations. In cooking, a breadmaking machine is an example of an active externalized artifact, whereas a spoon is a passive externalized one.

Some aspects of practice can be made **explicit**. They can be formulated in guidelines and theories. Cookbook recipes, textbooks about food and nutrition, dictionaries for chefs, and books about organizing work in big or small kitchens present examples of the explicit practice of cooking. They represent the articulable aspects of practice.

We can, however, only through practical experience learn the difference between a hand-mixed cake or a machine-mixed one, the difference between using four large eggs or four smaller ones, between an oven that is warm or an oven that is cold. Likewise can we learn the exact result of asking the kitchen assistant for three ripe tomatoes, or how to know when a certain steak cooked a certain way is "medium" as ordered by the customer. Only through practical experience do we operationalize actions, so that later the right operations will be triggered by the right conditions, for example, to choose a fork or a whisk to beat the eggs for a certain omelet. We call these aspects **personal** or **tacit**.[26]

Building up a repertoire of actions and operations is one result of learning and socialization into a group of human beings, such as a group of skilled workers' collective practice. But to master practice means not just to be able to carry out certain operations in which certain artifacts and languages are applied. Practice reflects both the instrumental and the communicative sides of actions and activities, and it reflects both the operational and the intentional aspects. To master practice means to know the meaning of, or the intentions behind, the words and the way of organizing work. An apprentice needs to know not only how the work is organized and how products come into being with this or that way of organizing work but also what it means if the master journeyman asks the apprentice to do something, compared to if a fellow apprentice does. The secretary needs to know how to approach, in writing and speaking, people at different levels at the workplace, and in its surroundings. This includes knowledge of the general rules and norms of the specific organization, and of the individuals around the secretary.

It is important not only to carry out some specific operations and actions to create a specific product from certain materials and with certain artifacts, but also to distinguish the quality of the materials, to know a good product from a bad one, and so forth. For a carpenter who is to make a dining table, the meanings of the words *oak* or *teak* denote not only two different kinds of wood, but also certain styles of products, certain artifacts and operations, and so on. To the secretary, a letter to the chairperson of the board and a draft of next year's budget imply different styles of writing as well as different typography and layout. It is through the intentional aspects that such matters as the quality of materials and products become communicable among human beings who share the same practice, not because each individual is able to make explicit the choices that were made and the reasons for these, but because they share values and experiences.

We can return to the example of Smalltalk-80. What does it mean to master the practice of Smalltalk-80 programming? First of all, it means to possess a repertoire of operations and actions, as previously discussed. Second, it means to know many legends about the history of the system, the work of its developers, and their ideas behind the system, such as Alan Kay's original Dynabook concept.[27] It means to know the structure of the system and the programming style that is part of the tradition.

Reading books about Smalltalk-80 and about programming and programming languages in general and working with the group of skilled Smalltalkers, watching what they do, studying examples, and trying things out oneself are all part of this mastery. To talk about Smalltalk-80 and to know the special vocabulary connected to this is important too. Goldberg explains some of this: "Some people refer to selection using a click as **bugging**. Their expressions take the form of 'bug that command' or 'bug outside the view'."[28]

To master Smalltalk-80 programming means to know the tradition, conventions and style; to recognize good Smalltalk-80 programming style when encountered; to know the programming styles that are applied by Smalltalkers, to use visual programming, to start out from how one wants things to look on the screen, to know how to start out by copying and modifying pieces of code that does "almost what one wants", without writing new code, and to know "debugging into existence," a way of creating pieces of code one-by-one when they are needed.

Some of this competence is explicit, such as some of the history and folklore, the programming language and the structure of the system.[29] Other parts are personal, such as knowing good programming style. And one doesn't find ones way through the system by remembering its structure explicitly but by knowing, by experience, that a method that looks almost like the needed one is hidden in some specific class in the hierarchy. The cultural techniques used in the programming activity are the programming style, the interaction style (such as the way we activate menus by pressing the buttons of the mouse), and the language by which we communicate about Smalltalk-80 programs.

The communicative and the instrumental sides

The communicative side as well as the instrumental side of human activity consist of operations and actions. What exists on the instrumental side in a certain combination of actions realized through operations triggered by the appearance of the material conditions is on the communicative side a combination of actions realized through operations triggered by communicative actions and operations conducted by another human being.[30] This encounter will be mediated by language but perhaps also by artifacts, such as telephones. The interpretation of the utterances is based both on practices of the communication partners, which they share to some extent, and on the actual operational setting surrounding the communication, for example whether one can give orders to the other or not.

The objects and subjects that we direct our actions and operations toward are not only nature, they are created out of culture. With subjects we share some practice, and only in rare occasions do we meet another human being as nature, as an object, toward which none of our communicative practice works. Good examples are difficult to come up with, but the situation where a sophisticated lady tries to explain to a hunter from a tribe in a remote corner of the world that her dog wants to "go to the bathroom" could end up as one example, because it is unlikely that the hunter has a bathroom, knows what it is, not to mention understands the idea of why a dog needs a bathroom and not just a tree.

In our relationship with things, we often meet artifacts, man-made things. Artifacts are not meant to be objects of our work but to mediate our relation with other objects. Artifacts can be the object for our actions and operations if these aim at producing the artifact, but the artifacts can also become nature to us another way if our operations stop working. In such total breakdowns we will no longer recognize a hammer but only pieces of wood and metal. To me, most mechanical devices, such as my car, stop being anything but pieces of metal and plastic the moment they stop working.

Learning

Learning is to socialize into the practice of a group through both reading of theory and practical experience. In this process, a person is not necessarily able to reproduce all aspects of practice. We can say that her personal competence level has not yet reached the level of an expert who masters a specific practice, with respect to that specific practice. Learning is also for a group to transcend this practice.[31]

An important part of learning in work is to build up a repertoire of operations. When a new artifact is brought into a practice this practice will change. Even the most competent expert will probably have to change her repertoire of operations, and for a while she is returning to a lower level of competence.[32] For this reason it is important to know how we learn to use a new artifact and how this differs from the routine use activity. Furthermore, it is important to know what impacts this difference has for design of the artifact.[33]

We can summarize investigations and discussions in the human activity literature[34] about how human beings learn, more specifically how they develop their repertoires of operations, as follows:

1. Activity on material objects cannot be learned without practical experience.

2. Activity that has an abstract goal, such as solving a mathematical problem, is easier learned[35] and carried out in connection with physical objects than with representations of such. Learning with representations is in turn easier than in connection with language, which is easier than activity that is totally based on mental reflection. For example, adding is first performed by children by counting physical objects, then they move on to master adding based on figures, then to a state where adding works best if they are allowed to talk, and so forth.

3. When operationalization takes place, it is at first very situation specific, but as the human being meets new conditions, the variation of situations that can be handled by operations grows.

4. For the novice, the activity takes place at a very detailed level of actions, where each action is consciously planned. With experience, the human being moves toward an operationalized totality. This is achieved through generalization, through operationalization of planned actions, and through abbreviation, an operationalized skipping of certain operations due to the conditions for them and a knowledge about the result. For example, in multiplication, when the result of multiplication by one is known

instead of having to carry out the operation, in communication, when the context is obvious to both communication partners; in carpentry when sandpapering is not necessary to smooth the wood because you already did well with the plane.

5. The person is brought down from one level of competence to another either due to some pedagogical questioning of the former operations and their conditions or because she is trying to apply old operations to the new artifact and is encountering a breakdown. If, and how fast, she can be brought back to her old level of competence or beyond depends on the artifact, on how much she can rely on the generality of her operations, on the type of education given, and on whether she can make use of experiences from other types of activity.

6. The use of an artifact is, if the artifact works well, operationalized. Ideally, learning starts out with actions toward the artifact and ends without those actions.

The challenge for design of the artifact is to build on existing work practice to avoid turning all experienced users into novices, both in their more general practice of the activity and in the specific use of the artifact. Furthermore, design changes practice by introducing the new artifact, but practice can also be influenced through education: The challenge is to design the needed education to change practice to make use of the new artifact. Design is a process of learning for the participants, that is, if competent users take part in design, both their general practice and their specific practice in relation to the future artifact change while the activity is going on.

We move on in the next section to more elaboration on the theory. The next issues are the computer-based artifact, and especially the user interface–what can we say about these issues using the theoretical background?

Computer applications

In this section, we shift focus from human activity to computer-based artifacts used in human activity. I use the human activity theory in an attempt to develop a framework of my own that allows for focus on the computer-based artifact. The idea is to develop a conception of computer-based artifacts, especially user interfaces, that can be applied in design. Such a conception is not necessarily recognizable by the user in a specific use situation: It belongs to the domain of computer application design. In this domain, the computer application is an object for the activity. In the domain of use, the specific computer-based artifacts have a meaning just like other artifacts we work with, as artifacts, not as objects that we work on.

I first discuss artifacts in general and then the characteristics specific to computer-based artifacts as compared to other artifacts. Finally, I discuss how we can define concepts such as user *interface*. I stressed in the introduction that these words have very different meanings in the literature, and I want in the following to give a definition that is operational from a design perspective.

When shifting the focus from the human activity to the artifacts themselves, we need a different vocabulary. I no longer talk about the user's activity, its object or goal, intentions, actions and operations, but about artifacts–the type of human activity that they (are intended to) support, the kind of practice they are part of, and so on.

Artifacts

Artifacts are things that mediate the actions of a human being toward another subject or toward an object. When we employ artifacts we direct actions and operations both toward the artifact and toward the subject or object, toward which we direct actions through the artifact. In situations where an action can be seen as communicative, some of the operations that realize it can be instrumental and vice versa.

As artifacts are not themselves objects for the activity, users are normally not meant to conduct action toward the artifacts. Both Leontjew and Polanyi[36] give examples of this for human activities such as reading, shooting, and hammering. Furthermore, the Smalltalk-80 example is an illustration of this. Because artifacts are not intended to be objects, we cannot use a hammer or talk about using a hammer without the real object in mind–driving a nail into a piece of wood. To the users, artifacts are what they are meant for.

Artifacts have traditionally evolved in a very slow process, taking years. Traditionally, the designer has been a competent craftsman, and there has been a close relationship between the designers and the users such that feedback from use has repeatedly led to new steps in design.[37]

Computer-based artifacts

Computer-based artifacts are developed much faster. They are complex and require the cooperation of different kinds of specialists. The designers are seldomly competent members of the future user community, and there is often no feedback from the users, because designers move on to new projects within other application domains. Furthermore,[38] they are not even experts in design, that is, they do not all possess the repertoire of operations to handle design, thus they tend to try and follow design methods as recipes instead.

Computer applications are inherently active externalized, and they can be applied to take over what were formerly human operations. In actual computer applications, this can be exploited to different extents. In many cases, computer-based artifacts, as compared to traditional artifacts, allow no direct access to the subject or object of the actions conducted through the artifact. We cannot see, hear, or feel the subject or object directly, only indirectly through the representation given by the computer. Often, the object does not even exist as something separate from the artifact: The messages that we create in an electronic mail system are only intended to exist as part of the computer application. It is part of human capabilities that we are able to project our experiences with one object onto another object or to couple these two types of experiences. Just like a blind person who is using a stick to 'see' the surroundings when walking the street, we can couple our experiences with the computer application with the real object and vice versa. Subjects do not need to be present in time either, the meeting between two subjects can be a meeting of one subject with some part of the computer application as a stand-in for the other subject.[39] This relationship gives computer applications a certain flexibility because it is easy to make the same computer application mediate the relation between the user and several different subjects or objects. The computer application becomes the artifact of several different activities and shifts between objects/subjects become part of what the user does while applying the computer application.

The point here is not to say that all computer-based artifacts are very different from traditional artifacts but to say that they can be very different even though they play the same role in use as the traditional ones. When we shift from talking about a specific use activity to talking about a specific artifact we can no longer talk about one object, one repertoire of operations, and so on. Instead, we must talk about a number of goals or objects or a certain type of goals or objects, about certain types of objects and subjects on which the users of the artifact can conduct certain actions, and so forth. Without a specific use situation in front of us, we can only talk about intentions. Computer-based artifacts are intended to support a specific type of use activity. They arise out of and are intended for a specific practice. They arise out of various other conditions for this type of use activity.

In a specific use activity, where the artifact is applied, the user can perform some action on some object through the artifact, other actions on some other object or subject, and still others on the artifact as an object. Some of these actions can belong to the communicative side of human activity and others to the instrumental. Traditionally, some artifacts are primarily intended to support the instrumental side and other the communicative side. For many computer applications this distinction is less clear because they often mediate actions and operations toward both objects and subjects.

The user interface

By supporting certain specific actions, the computer-based artifact supports both intentional and operational aspects–*what* can be done by means of the artifact and *how* it can be done. Traditionally, we often denote the intentional aspects of a computer application as the *functionality–what* can be done by means of the application. The use of this type of concept belongs to a different theoretical tradition than the human activity approach, an approach where human activity is conceived as consciously planned action: Everything is consciously planned and every step in use is consciously taken. With the human activity approach, the functionality can be seen as something that only reveals itself in breakdowns and situations of reflection. In such situations, it is possible to focus on properties of the results of the use process–on what was done–presupposing a situation of use.

The conditions for the operational aspects that are given by the computer application are called the *user interface*. The user interface is the artifact-bound conditions for *how* actions can be done. Constituent parts of this interface can be conditions both for operations directed toward the artifact and for operations directed toward the real objects or subjects at different levels. This way, I define **human–computer interaction** as human operation of a computer application.

We can look at an example to show how the human being changes the subject/object and, thus, the level of action during the use of an artifact.

A person, Anne, is using a word processor (Fig. 2.5) to write a document to be read by some other person, Betty. Anne is, of course, writing the document for Betty, and she will try to explain things to Betty to make her understand. Betty is the subject for this type of action. The action can be realized both through operations directed toward the subject (Betty and Anne use certain words and phrases in their usual communication) and through operations directed toward the document or the word processor. Anne can, however, also direct actions toward the document: She can work on the form (e. g. the typography) or she can work on the language (e. g. on the syntax) without directly thinking of Betty.

Furthermore, we can imagine that Betty is a television newscaster and that the document Anne writes is her manuscript; or that Betty is answering questions from the readers of a newspaper and Anne is writing her. In both cases, Anne, while writing the document, will probably also think of communicating with the viewers or readers–she will direct actions toward these subjects, too.

But we can imagine still other objects toward which she directs her actions, for example, actions directed toward the word processor. Anne will either conduct actions toward the word processor if she has not yet developed the repertoire of operations needed for what she wants to achieve or if a breakdown occurs, like a space key not working well.

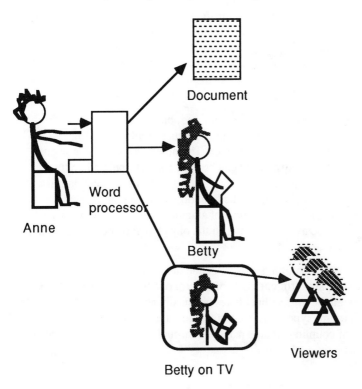

Figure 2.5. Anne using the artifact

In the example as well as in general, the user interface supports actions toward the different objects and subjects that the user is intended to deal with through the artifact. But the artifact as such is transparent in the sense that it should not be an object for the actions of the user in regular use.

Breakdowns can occur for many other reasons than just an unsuitable user interface. Material conditions other than the computer application can cause the breakdown, and even when we talk about the computer application such things as software and hardware errors can cause breakdowns. In the worst case, a user will see the word processor as some boxes and moving parts. How is it possible to be more specific when talking about what it means for a user to handle an object in or through the artifact or when communicating with another human being through the artifact? We can make the following distinctions among different types of situations:

1. The object is present only in the artifact (Fig. 2.6). An example of this is a spreadsheet, which has no direct relation to objects outside the artifact (a printout of a spreadsheet does not have the same capabilities as the spreadsheet). The quality of the user interface must, for this type of artifact, deal with whether the user can distinguish between handling of the artifact and handling of the object in the artifact.

2. The object exists as a physical object, too, but is only present in the use activity as the representation in the computer application (Fig. 2.7). An example of this is a word processor: The object is a letter that is only present in the use activity as what can be seen and manipulated on the screen. The quality of the user interface for this type of application must relate to how the user can couple the final object and the object on the screen to each other. This is the type of situation where we can view parts of the user interface as a filter between the object as it is present in the use activity and the real object.

3. The object is present, physically, outside the artifact (Fig. 2.8). Examples of this are different kinds of control panels, where the object is handled through the artifact but also is physically accessible for inspection. For this type of user interface, too, the quality relates to the possibilities of coupling what is achieved through the artifact with what is happening with the real object.

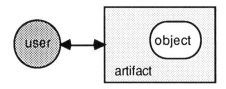

Figure 2.6. The object is present only in the artifact

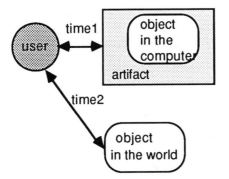

Figure 2.7. The object exists as a physical object, but is only present in the use activity as the representation in the computer application.

Applications similar to types 2 and 3 exist for the support of the communicative side:

4. The other subject is not physically present in the use activity. An example of this is a mail system. Here, too, it must be possible for the user to make the coupling between how the other subject is experienced through the artifact and the subject.

5. The subjects are physically present but communicate (partially) through the artifact. Examples of such applications can be found in the ideas of the Xerox Co-lab project.[40]

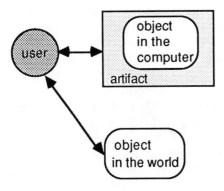

Figure 2.8. The object is physically present outside the artifact.

Later I go into more detail about how we can understand the user interface and the role of the user interface in use. I have chosen to characterize different aspects of the user interface based on the distinction between the different objects/subjects toward which the human being directs her operations, and on the specific role and characteristics of these subjects/objects in use. I distinguish among:

a. The **physical aspects**, the support for our operations toward the computer application as a physical object. We will meet this object in the total breakdown or before we get to know the application. The physical aspects are the conditions for the physical handling of the artifact. The human adapts to the forms and shapes of the artifact, and a maladaption might prevent the forming of certain operations.[41]

b. The **handling aspects**,[42] the support for operations toward the computer application. A breakdown in these operations will make the artifact appear to us as an object. The handling aspects are the conditions for the transparency of the artifact. As the artifact is a thing, the operations that are supported are inherently instrumental, no matter whether the actions are communicative or instrumental. In breakdown situations, for example, this kind of operations can be conceptualized, whereby the user can be forced to conduct actions toward the artifact as an object.

c. The **subject/object-directed aspects** that constitute the conditions for operations directed toward objects or subjects that we deal with in the artifact or through the artifact. Different parts of the subject/object-directed aspects relate to different subjects or objects, but it is also part of these aspects to support the shift between subjects/objects.

The physical aspects might seem more tangible or manifest than the others, which might suggest that they have a different status than the other aspects. This is true in one way–the physical aspects constitute the nature that we can feel, see, and hear in the total breakdown. Culturally, however, all three aspects are dependent on practice. For the competent user, all aspects are equally present in a specific use activity: They constitute a totality and a possibility of shifts between aspects.[43] Taking the example of a word processor, it is only in the most total breakdown situations that the word processor can be reduced to wire and plastic. The outsiders who do not share this practice will recognize a bunch of buttons, a visual display terminal, and so on, not because they are something special but because we all share a common culture or practice as modern human beings in our contemporary society.[44]

Let's once again take a look at Anne–how do the different aspects of the user interface of the word processor support or influence her actions and operations? A breakdown at the physical level occurs if the space key is not working well. The handling aspects support her building of operations so that she is working on a letter or writing to Betty, not just pressing buttons. Breakdowns occur from different other levels of focus (focus on Betty, on the letter, on the viewers) if the word processor responds to her actions and operations in a way that Anne is not used to or not expecting. Not only could there be software or hardware errors, but there could also be some prompts that needs to be answered before she can proceed.[45] Depending on which part of the activity we consider (Anne's action directed toward Betty, toward the document, or toward the viewers or readers), we will see different parts of the subject/object-directed aspects: The way that the document is displayed on the screen and Anne's possibilities of giving the document the needed layout have to do with actions and operations toward the document as well as with Anne's possibilities of forgetting the document and writing for Anne instead.

We can imagine, for example, that a simple line-oriented editor will help express Anne's thoughts toward Betty in just the way she likes, but only in capital letters. But in the end, the signals that she sends to Betty are, of course, also a result of her possibilities of actions or operations toward the other objects or subjects. Breakdowns can occur when Anne is focusing on the viewers–"Betty wouldn't want to read this . . ."–and her focus is on Betty. If she focuses on Betty, a sudden misspelling or hopeless layout might cause her to focus on the letter, and so on.

Physical and handling aspects are conditions for possible operations toward the artifact and actions toward the subject/object. And, subject/object-directed aspects added to this are conditions for possible operations toward the subject or object. In the actual use situation, breakdowns can occur between any two subjects/objects, and an operation toward one subject/object might be a prerequisite for an action or operation toward another. The aspects as such are independent of each other, but one piece of software or hardware can constitute several parts of the aspects, as illustrated in Fig. 2.9–the way a document is displayed to Anne can be a condition for both forgetting about the artifact and for thinking about the layout of the letter. Furthermore, breakdowns in a certain sense propagate upward: If the mouse is broken, it is hard to think about editing text, and so forth.

The user interface only reveals itself fully to us in use. How we can handle this challenge in design is discussed in the next section.

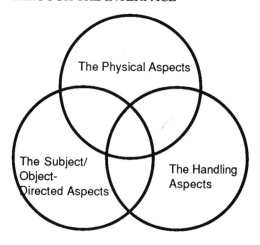

Figure 2.9. Software and hardware contributing to the different aspects of the user interface

Design

In this section I look briefly at computer application design seen as an anthropological phenomenon. A short discussion of design and design practice as conceived by means of the framework is given. This presentation is further elaborated upon in Chapter 5. The first look is at the relationship between use and design of computer applications. This is followed by a discussion of design practice, and finally, the special area of the user interface is discussed.

The ideas of this section are inspired by the work of Winograd and Flores, Ehn,[46] and others, perhaps even more than it is inspired by the human activity theory. However, I have found arguments for the following points in the human activity theory as well.

Design of computer-based artifacts

A unfulfilled **need** is the origin for design as for any other activity. However, in our society this need is not necessarily the common need of the group of users and other involved parties. Most often, computer applications are designed to fulfill the needs of managers of the use organization. Design takes place within organizational frames that tie groups with different interests together by means of power and resources.[47] Throughout the design process, many decisions and choices are made, which are not always based on rationality but often on experience or practice of the group and on bargaining or negotiations between the involved groups of interest.[48] The needs of the most powerful parties often drive design in a direction away from seeing and designing the product as an artifact. The purpose of this section is to state conditions under which design of computer-based artifacts can take place.

Design of artifacts is a process[49] by which we determine and create the conditions that turn an object into an artifact of use. The future use situation is the origin for design, and we design with this in mind. Use, as a process of learning, is a prerequisite to design. Through use, new needs arise, either as a result of changing conditions of work or as a recognition of problems with the present artifacts through recurring breakdowns. The power relations and the division of labor are important factors for what kind of needs eventually leads to design activities and implemented artifacts.

To design with the future use activity in mind also means to start out from the present practice(s) of the future users. It is through their experiences that the need for design has arisen, and it is their practice that is to be applied and changed in the future use activity.[50] Design of computer-based artifacts is a meeting place for many different practices, where sharing experiences is something that requires a deliberate effort. *Design is a process of learning*, both when viewed as a collective process and as an individual process for the participants. The different groups involved learn about the practices of the other participating groups. For the computer experts,[51] this involves learning about the work and prerequisites of the application domain. For the users who participate, learning about computers is combined with learning about design of computer applications. For all groups, the encounter with practices of other groups contributes to learning about one's own practice, which also lends a creative aspect to design: Possibilities for new ways of doing things that transcend the traditional practices of the users.

Design is based on and may change all aspects of the practices of the users. Conceptualization, the process of bringing into our consciousness the nature of our practice, takes place in different situations and is *triggered* by different means. In design, we need the means with which to trigger awareness of all aspects of practice while we also need to realize that some of the personal or tacit aspects of practice are better dealt with without conceptualization. In this process, two potentially conflicting goals of design come into play: that the future users must be able to assess the artifact-to-be and that the programmers need a formal and detailed basis for their programming. This potential conflict can be dealt with in two ways: either to let the users be as detailed and explicit about their requirements as possible or to provide the programmers with the needed competence to take part in design and help transform breakdowns into actual programs. The human activity framework tells us that the first way is hardly feasible alone. The second way emphasizes the need for a collective learning process among the groups involved in design. Furthermore, to be a good designer means to be able to facilitate reflection and transformation in breakdown situations.

Although triggering conceptualization is important in design, design rarely aims at creating chaos or the total breakdown. Each activity in design has a purpose in relation to the goal of the design activity: to achieve a design of an artifact that fulfills its purpose in use. Sharing a practice makes it possible to pursue this line, whereas we can say that conceptualization and breakdowns adjust individual participants' reflection regarding the future artifacts to each other and to reality.

Any action of use of the artifact has both intentional and operational aspects. Design will often start from the intentional aspects because these become conscious to us in breakdowns, and we are directly capable of communicating about our intentions. To fully understand the artifact, we must, however, start out from the use activity. This is the only way to focus also on the operational aspects of use, and thus on the user interface and the artifact *in use*.

To design an artifact means more than designing the object that can be used by human beings as artifacts in a specific kind of activity. As the use of artifacts is part of social activity, we *design new conditions for collective activity*, for example, new divisions of labor and other new ways of coordination, control, and communication. Design of education is important, too, because the artifact is to be integrated into an existing practice. This integration changes not only the operational aspects of the artifact but also the other aspects of practice (goals, purposes). A good education can facilitate this change.

Computers are capable of replacing human operations. In the design of an actual computer-based artifact, however, this fact can play a more or less dominant role, depending on the design strategy and the application domain. The key thing to remember is that it is possible to choose to automate previous operations from the specific activity, or one could choose to avoid such automation. A traditional accounting system is an example of a computer application where automation is important. Previously, the human would do the calculation, now one just enters numbers and the machine does the calculation. The same is true of traditional CNC-lathes (computer numerical control) and many other applications. With modern document preparation applications, or with many modern CNC-machines, it is a different matter. Of course, certain former human operations are applied, such as the use of addition for bringing up the document. However, the important aspects are that the user can enter text, design and change layout, and so on, in an even more flexible way than with a typewriter, but with the same feeling of control.

Practice of designers

In this section I focus on the practice of designers, with particular emphasis on different means of triggering conceptualization in design of a computer-based artifact. The discussion of concrete means is saved for Chapter 5. Furthermore, I discuss the role of design methods in relation to the practice of the users.

Through conceptualization, we can either direct attention away from an existing or traditional[52] practice (artifacts, operations, and their material conditions) toward a new artifact or away from a new artifact toward a future use practice, especially new artifacts and the implications of such for operations and their triggering. We can distinguish two types of activities in which we make use of conceptualization: **investigation** activities, where we start from a practice to find out about a changed artifact, and **communication** activities, where new or changed artifacts are evaluated and a changed practice can be the result.

Conceptualization can be achieved through the use of artifacts and techniques by which we can construct a **materialized vision** of the future use activity, including the artifact. In other words, the mere creation, as well as the materialized visions serve as triggers. Examples of such triggers are scenario techniques, systems description techniques, and prototyping. Materialized visions are the means by which we try to fix and materialize ideas about different aspects of the future artifact at the same time as they are the means or points of reference for communication between groups and individuals involved in design. There are two goals of creating such materialized visions: the communication and the actual **construction**.

Other triggers are applied that can be very different from those mentioned. Some of these can build upon breakdowns achieved through reading, actual implementation of the use activity, or simulated implementation. There can also be more or less structured ways of being forced to reflect on one's own practice, especially actions and operations. An important aspect of such techniques is the connection between communication and investigation activities.

Design methods are means of changing the practice of designers. They are prescriptions for the use of certain design means aimed at a total design activity or at design activities with more specific goals as part of this. According to Mathiassen,[53] design methods prescribe the use of certain **artifacts, techniques,** and **principles of organization**[54] in correspondence with the cultural techniques, language, artifacts, and ways of organizing work that the designers apply as part of a design practice. The prescribed means, together with a more or less explicit application domain and perspective, are the results of some delineation of a practice: The methods are created or written down by designers who believe that they know good ways to design within a certain domain. In this process, important parts of their experiences get lost, and only the explicit parts of their competence are captured in the method; the design artifacts, but not all aspects of their use, and only the explicit parts of the cultural techniques are utilized. For the use of a method this has the consequence that a method is **not** a recipe to be followed step by step, like a computer executing a program, but rather a set of guidelines for a certain kind of activity to be learned by the designers and later applied through the repertoire of actions and operations.

This is only acknowledged in very few methods. Instead, many authors claim a certain generality of their methods because they forget to make the application domain explicit. Furthermore, many have the attitude "Follow my method and you'll be happy." Authors of methods can, of course, be blamed for this attitude. On the other hand, analyzers of design methods often have the same attitude: that by following the method step by step we should be able to achieve what the author claims to have achieved through practice. Both the authors and the critics forget the importance of encountering the actual material conditions and of learning.

One dilemma is that methods often aim at compensating for lack of competence: By suggesting a certain way of organizing work and the use of certain means of design it is claimed that the designers need a smaller amount of design competence. But with less competence, as with all other kinds of human labor activity, the designers' repertoire of operations and actions has repercussions on the quality of the product,[55] because they cannot fully act according to the situation encountered.

Design of user interfaces

In this section I summarize and elaborate on some important statements about the design of user interfaces.

In design we must deal with articulated, nonarticulated, and nonarticulable aspects of practice and with conceptualization in relation to these aspects. In this connection, the user interface is a special challenge: Operations as such can be conceptualized and made specific by various means, for example, by writing the operations down or by teaching others what to do. However, *the conditions that trigger a certain operation from the repertoire of operations are what we need to investigate in user interface design.* The actual triggering of **one** combination of actions and operations compared to another is part of the personal competence. This means that only breakdowns can draw attention to the triggering and the actual conditions. By using the repertoire of operations under different circumstances, such as different user interfaces and different materials or communication situations, the occurrence of a breakdown can be tested and the conditions for the choice of operations revealed. The physical aspects as well as the handling and the subject/object-directed aspects of the user interface are examined only through actual use situations.

The user interface creates the conditions by which the artifact does not object to the activity toward the real subjects or objects of the activity. Design is a process that leads from a situation of numerous ways of conceptualizations, about the earlier artifacts, about practice, and so forth, to a situation where the artifacts don't cause breakdowns and where it is possible to create the needed repertoire of actions and operations toward the object or subject.

The human activity approach: Summary, relations and constraints

I have now presented the theory underlying this book and my own approach. I have chosen to call this a *human activity approach to user interface design*. This approach takes its starting point in human activity and allows us to deal with both communication and relations to objects as aspects of this activity. Using this approach, computers can be considered anthropologically as belonging to the same category as other artifacts.

Human activity is part of the social activity of various groups and it has a purpose that contributes to the goal of the collective activity. The person is part of the practice of the group. Human activity is also a personal activity. To conduct a certain activity, the person has a repertoire of operations that are applied in conscious actions. While an activity is being carried out, certain shifts in levels of action occur due to conceptualization and operationalization.

Each action performed by a human being has not only intentional aspects but also operational aspects. Likewise, the artifacts employed in the actions support these aspects. When the person uses some computer-based artifact in this activity, the most fundamental level of operation is an adaptation to the physical aspects of the user interface. In addition, the handling aspects serve to operate the artifact. And the subject/object-directed aspects support the development and use of a repertoire of operations toward subjects or objects through the application.

We have discussed how practice is important when applying, introducing, and designing artifacts particularly the consequences of this for design of computer-based artifacts. In design we face a number of potential conflicts: Computers are inherently active externalized artifacts but sometimes we want to design computer applications that are passive externalized. Design is a social activity in which we need to communicate about operational aspects of the instrumental side of human activity. Design of user interfaces means the conceptualization of former operations as well as the creation of conditions for new operations.

I have argued that design means dealing with the practices of the involved groups. Design is fundamentally a collective activity, in which the various practices of the participants meet in a process of mutual learning. This meeting creates conflicts that create new possibilities in design.

This approach is an approach to design of artifacts for human work. No attempts have been made to claim generality of the approach outside this area. At the same time, this is an indirect critique of most of the traditional human factors research. In order to avoid dealing with the difficult questions of competence and learning in connection with the user interface–questions that the human activity approach considers essential–these researchers make a number of assumptions that lead them to only consider casual users and novices. These casual users and novices are not as much people who have never, or rarely, seen the actual device before, but rather they are nonskilled workers in a certain trade (e. g., word processors are often tested on college students, not on secretaries). For this reason, hardly any existing research about good user interfaces for office automation are applicable in design based on the human activity approach, because all the research is the result of letting students or other novices, not professional office workers, try out the equipment. The human activity approach allows for a definition of the user interface by which we can focus on different use aspects of the user interface. Furthermore, the definition stresses that competence within the application domain is important for the user interface, in its design as well as in its utilization. For example, as a computer scientist visiting a trade show, I am not able to see the user interface of a page makeup system the way competent typographers who have been taught to use the system in their daily work do. The definition of a user interface is not a purely technical or mechanical one. Neither is it purely individualistic, that is, it is not a definition that claims that the user interface is different for each individual who comes into contact with the application. For design, such a definition would hardly be operational unless we also accepted the assumption that we could never design artifacts except for individuals. Such an assumption goes against our anthropological view of how artifacts have been developed through history.

This, on the other hand, is not the same as saying that we cannot make user interfaces adjustable to individual needs.

One of the potential problems of the approach is its close relationship to that between language and the organization of instrumental work: It can be argued that due to the division of labor in our society, a certain kind of work exists that has hardly anything to do with instrumental work and the production of tangible products. Rather, this work has to do with a reproduction of knowledge within the organization[56] and with communication for its own sake. In the framework of Leontjew, we can see such activity as activity that, due to the division of labor, has goals that have to do with maintenance and reproduction of the cultural techniques, ways of coordinating, and communication about work as part of the organization's total collective activity.

The main limitation to the approach in my view is its lack of focus on gender issues. I have searched through the human activity literature for discussions of specific male or female aspects of life. I did not find any, which to a certain extent accounts for the lack of such discussion here. Furthermore there is a problem of translation. The English translations of Leontjew's work, which are different than the Danish translations, use the terms *man* and *men's work* instead of the less gender specific words *human beings* and *human work*.[57] The Danish translations are for the most parts also much more readable, thus I often found it necessary to retranslate terms from Danish into English.

A narrow interpretation of skills and competence in Leontjew's work creates problems, because it leads to a definition of skills and competence as something possessed by the traditional craftsman. A wider interpretation–that competence or skill has to do with the extent to which a human being master a certain practice, a social practice dealing with the relationship among human beings, as well as a practice where relationships to artifacts and materials are important–also covers the type of skills that women are likely to possess. Furthermore, I think that the approach is particularly relevant to gender values in design.[58] The approach stresses that everyday life and practice are the origins of design and that human needs, not technical problems or fixes, foster design.

I have interpreted Leontjew's work in other ways as well, in ways that are significantly different than others in the literature. Leontjew, and his successors, argued that operations could be automated by a machine:[59] "It is generally the fate of operations that, sooner or later, they become a function of a machine."[60] In my interpretation, this means that the human being, through actions and operations, activates a machine, whereas it is still up to the human being to assess the material conditions. Some authors took a different stance and used the statement in an attempt to develop artificial intelligence,[61] achieving what I feel is a conflicting purpose, because they end up in discussions similar to those of cognitive science. The discussions conclude with how we can articulate as much as necessary of the material conditions for the operations and thereby we make machines that fully take over human operations. This view is closely related to the tendency in Marxist thinking to consider so-called scientific or theoretical knowledge (i. e. breakdown knowledge) as superior or more profound than everyday knowledge or practice.[62] In my opinion, these are both necessary if we want to design in keeping with existing practice, while also desiring the possibility of changing this.

I have made only one restriction on the application domain of the human activity approach in this chapter: that it deals with computer support for purposeful human work. However, it is clear that the theoretical approach carries with it the assumption that computer support for purposeful human work is artifacts. Depending on how we interpret this, we can turn the assumption into a constraint of the application domain or a perspective on quality. The statement about the application domain is that we only deal with computer applications that can be seen as artifacts for human work, that is, there might be other computer applications for human work activity that are not intended to be artifacts. To turn this into a statement about perspective, we can say that we conceive human work activity as supported by artifacts, that is, computer applications that are to function well in human work activity must be applicable as artifacts.

To ponder the question of the generality of the human activity approach, we can negate the two statements and ask which computer applications are used in purposeful human work but do not mediate the human being's relationship with other human beings or to the physical world? Random number generators and different kinds of simulators are candidates because they produce some result without any direct connection to the material world. However, it is difficult to come up with any concrete examples of this. In the different examples I can think of, the random number generator is hidden in some other application that is an artifact to its user, or in the simulator case, the purpose is to communicate some (physical) experiences from one person to another. As a paradox, such an example would be no problem, because this computer application, as an object, would need no user interface in the sense that this concept has been developed here.

In the following chapters I use and elaborate on this approach along two lines: In Chapter 4, we go into more detail about the user interface, to use the framework to characterize user interfaces and to reach some qualitative statements about user interfaces.

In Chapter 5, we use the approach to study how various design methods view the computer-based artifact, and more specifically, the user interface. We see what types of design activities and user interfaces come out of the use of the design artifacts and techniques that the methods prescribe. There are three main areas in Chapter 5: a framework by which to characterize design methods and their view of user interfaces; an assessment of the cognitive science tradition; and a discussion of the possibilities of a new and better design approach.

---

[1] Winograd, T., & Flores C. F. (1986). *Understanding computers and cognition: A new foundation for design.* Norwood, NJ: Ablex.

2 MacPaint is the Apple Macintosh standard program for free-hand drawing (see Macintosh MacPaint, Apple Computers Inc. M1502).

[3] Oberquelle, H., Kupka, I., & Maass, S. (1983). A view of human–machine communication and cooperation. *International Journal of Man–Machine Studies, 19(4)*, 309–333.

[4] See, for example, Ehn, P., & Kyng, M. (1984). A tool perspective on design of interactive computer support for skilled workers. In M. Sääksjärvi (Ed.), *Proceedings from the Seventh Scandinavian Research Seminar on Systemeering* (pp. 211–242). Helsinki: Helsinki Business School or Shiel, B. (1983). Power tools for programmers. *Datamation, 29(2)*, 131-144.

5 Both communication and interaction indicate some kind of equality in communication between the parties involved. I would like to emphasize this connotation and ideally choose a different word to cover what I am after. The concepts are, however, both well established for "what goes on between the human being and the computer." Thus, instead of introducing a new concept, I prefer to use the term human–computer interaction throughout this book. However, I stress that this usage does not indicate any kind of a priori resemblance with interpersonal communication.

[6] Carroll, J. (1989a). *Evaluation, description, and invention: Paradigms for human–computer interaction* (RC 13926 [#62583]). Yorktown Heights, N.Y.: IBM.

[7] I use the concept artifact to stress that computer applications are made by human beings, they are culture as opposed to nature. In my use this is synonymous with such words as tool, medium, device, means, although this meaning is not connected to the word artifact in its traditional meaning. The problems with such words as tool, medium, etc., are that they are used within different traditions (see Chapter 5), that they are each more specific than the word I need, and that they do not as directly imply that tools, media, etc., are made by human beings. I use the concept computer application as the generic term for some collection of software and hardware that is applied together for some purpose. I try to avoid the use of the term computer-based system unless I explicitly deal with a computer application that is designed from a systems perspective (see Chapter 5).

[8] Although it is in line with the fundamental perspective of the present book, this choice entails that the results about user interfaces might not hold for casual use of computers, computers for leisure, computers in education, etc.

[9] Leontjew, A. N. (1981b). *Problems of the development of the mind.* Moscow: Progress or Leontjew, A. N. (1978). *Activity, consciousness, and personality.* Englewood Cliffs, NJ: Prentice-Hall.

[10] Hydén, L.-C. (1981). *Psykologi och materialism. Introduktion till den materialistiska psykologin* [Psychology and materialism. An Introduction to materialistic psychology]. Stockholm: Prisma.

[11] Karpatschof, B. (1984). Grænsen for automatisering [The Limit of automation]. *Psyke og Logos, 2,* 201–220.

[12] Wittgenstein, L. (1953). *Philosophical investigations.* Oxford: Oxford University Press and Lundequist, J. (1982). *Norm och modell* [Norm and model]. Unpublished doctoral dissertation, The Royal Institute of Technology, Stockholm.

[13] Polanyi, M. (1967). *Personal knowledge.* London: Routledge & Kegan Paul.

[14] Winograd & Flores, op. cit. (note 1).

[15] The intention of this section is to give the reader the knowledge of the framework in which to place the rest of the book. A presentation like this cannot cover all aspects of a theory, thus the reader who wishes to know more is referred to my sources.

[16] Page makeup is the process through which newspaper pages are put together out of articles, ads, and pictures. For a description of page makeup see, for example, Bødker, S., Ehn, P., Kammersgaard, J., Kyng, M., & Sundblad, Y. (1987). A Utopian experience. In G. Bjerknes, P. Ehn, & M. Kyng (Eds.). *Computers and democracy: A Scandinavian challenge* (pp. 251–278). Aldershot, UK: Avebury.

[17] We face the problem here that it is difficult to talk about operations: When we name them we almost always talk about their intentions, that is we do not talk about the operations but about the similar actions.

[18] It is difficult to name all the sources that have inspired me. Notes in this and the following chapters give specific references. However, my main reference sources have been Leontjew, op. cit. (note 9), Hydén, op. cit. (note 10), and Karpatschof, op. cit. (note 11).

[19] Juul-Jensen, U. (1973) *Videnskabsteori* (Vol. 2) [The philosophy of science]. Copenhagen: Berlinske Forlag, my translation.

[20] Ibid.

[21] Fig. 2.1 is inspired by Hydén, op. cit. (note 10).

[22] The example used here is the overall example used in Goldberg, A. (1984). *SMALLTALK-80: The interactive programming environment.* Reading, MA:

Addison-Wesley. The example is presented on p. 10 pp and illustrates how one can program a class in Smalltalk-80 with which to manage one's personal finances. In the example, it is possible to enter transactions, keep track of those transactions, view the transactions in different ways by means of different Smalltalk views, etc.

[23] Leontjew, op. cit. (note 9) calls this automation, a term that I try to avoid because of its connotations of "automation by a computer" (see also note 59).

[24] Leontjew ibid. In the terminology introduced by Winograd & Flores, op. cit. (note 1), there are ready-to-hand and present-at-hand, which Winograd & Flores have adopted from Heidegger. The term breakdown is used to indicate the shift of our practice and artifacts from being ready-to-hand to being present-at-hand, similar to what Leontjew call conceptualization. I use the term breakdown only to indicate such shifts that are caused by some unpredicted conflict between the operation and its material conditions.

[25] This does not just mean that we don't talk about them, but also, that we are not aware of them nor distinguish among them.

[26] Wittgenstein, op. cit. (note 12) and Polanyi, op. cit. (note 13) talk about tacit knowledge: what we can act according to but not talk about. Furthermore, they make a distinction between what we usually don't talk about and what we cannot talk about. They see a difference between our everyday competence and scientific or theoretical competence, where everyday competence is more profound or richer than theoretical, because it includes nonarticulable aspects through the relation to the material world.

Theory arises from our everyday competence, but it cannot explain the full truth about the activity of human beings and about the conditions for this. Here we find the reasons for my initial statement about the usability of a theory: Applicability in use is the ultimate test of the theory.

Furthermore, general design methods and recommendations about the user interface can be useful in design of the artifact. However, we can not be certain of their usefulness before we have tried them out in the design activity. We can say that methods and recommendations can help us go in the right direction so as to avoid too many breakdowns in design, but we cannot be sure that we have made the right product before the users have tested it.

For a comparative discussion of different perspectives on the relation between practice and theoretical knowledge see Ehn, P. (1988). *Work-oriented design of computer artifacts*. Falköping, Sweden: Arbetslivscentrum/Almqvist & Wiksell International.

[27] See, for example Kay, A., & Goldberg, A. (1981). A personal dynamic media. In A. I. Wasserman (Ed.), *Software development environment* (pp. 82–92). New York: IEEE.

[28] Goldberg op cit. (note 22).

[29] Goldberg ibid. Also Goldberg, A., & Robson, D. (1983). *SMALLTALK-80: The language and its implementation*. Reading, MA: Addison-Wesley, and Krasner, G.

(Ed.) (1983). *SMALLTALK-80: Bits of history, words of advice*. Reading, MA: Addison-Wesley.

[30] This is a little simplified, because actions and operations toward objects can play a role in the communication too.

[31] The importance of this aspect for design is expanded upon in Engeström, Y. (1987). *Learning by expanding*. Helsinki: Orienta-Konsultit, Christiansen, E. (1989). *Den realistiske vision* [The realistic vision]. Unpublished doctoral dissertation, Ålborg Universitetscenter, Denmark, Bisgaard, O., Mogensen, P., Nørby, M., & Thomsen, M. (1989). *Systemudvikling som lærevirksomhed, konflikter som basis for organisationel udvikling* [Systems development as a learning activity, conflicts as the origin of organizational development] (DAIMI IR-88). Århus: University of Aarhus.

[32] Furthermore, Christiansen, ibid. stresses the importance of a changed understanding of work. Due to the HCI focus in this book, I do not deal specifically with this.

[33] This discussion is continued in Chapters 4 and 5. In Chapter 4, the focus is on how actual artifacts do or do not support learning. In Chapter 5, we look at how design methods deal with learning, and what the theory, on which this book builds, can tell us about the handling of practice and learning in design.

[34] Leontjew, op. cit. (note 9), Gal'perin, P. Y. (1969). Stages in the development of mental acts. In Cole, M., & Maltzman, I. (Eds.). *A handbook of contemporary Soviet psychology* (pp. 249-273), New York: Basic. Also Dreyfus, H., & Dreyfus, S. (1986). *Mind over machine: The power of human intuition and expertise in the era of the computer*. Glasgow: Basil Blackwell, make some observations about the nature of learning of actions and operations. Their example is discussed in Chapter 4.

[35] Gal'perin, ibid.

[36] Leontjew, op. cit. (note 9), and Polanyi, op. cit. (note 13).

[37] Göranzon, B., Gullers, P., Mäkilä, K., Svensson, P., & Thollander, L. (1983) *Datorn som verktyg–krav och ansvar vid systemutveckling* [The computer as a tool]. Lund: Studentlitteratur.

[38] Ibid.

[39] This is what Oberquelle et al., op. cit. (note 3) call delegation with a word borrowed from Petri. Other people and noncomputer-based artifacts can stand in for a person as well; secretaries or answering machines answering telephone calls are examples of this.

[40] See, for example, Stefik, M., Bobrow, D. G., Lanning, S., & Tatar, D. (1986). WYSIWIS revisited: Early experiences with multi-user interfaces. *Proceedings from CSCW '86*. (pp. 276–290) Conference on Computer-Supported Cooperative Work, December 3–5, 1986, Austin, Texas.

[41] The physical aspects are the conditions for what Leontjew calls psychological and physiological functions, which are the basic components of operations.

[42] According to Webster's new world dictionary, handling means to touch, lift, operate, etc., with the hand, to manage or control, but also to respond to control (e. g. the car handles well).

[43] Another example of this is a hammer: We all know what a hammer is, and nobody will probably claim that the most natural characteristics of a hammer are that it consists of a piece of metal and a piece of wood.

[44] It is true, however, that the software side is developing faster than the hardware side, which makes the physical aspects more stable than the other aspects, and, hence, the computers more recognizable for us than, say, text editors.

[45] See further examples in Chapter 4.

[46] Winograd & Flores, op. cit. (note 1) or Ehn, op. cit. (note 26).

[47] For a book like this one, we face the problem that the needs of managers do not necessarily include quality artifacts for the employees. We do, however, see more and more cases where quality is emphasized, and I see my contribution both as supporting such efforts with a theoretical foundation and concrete design methods and as pointing out prototypical cases where user interface design is done differently, and perhaps better.

[48] See Winograd & Flores, op. cit. (note 1), Dreyfus & Dreyfus, op. cit. (note 34), Mathiassen, L. (1981). *Systemudvikling og systemudviklingsmetode* [Systems development and systems development method] (DAIMI PB-136). Århus: University of Aarhus or Ehn, P., & Sandberg, Å. (1979). God utredning [Good investigation]. In Å. Sandberg (Ed.), *Utredning och förändring i förvaltningen,* (pp. 13-57). Stockholm: Liber.

[49] This is of course only true as long as we stay within the application domain of the theoretical approach. Design of a computer game, or of a piece of artwork, might not be covered by this conception of design.

[50] See Engeström, op. cit. (note 31) and Bisgaard et al., op cit. (note 31).

[51] I use designers to mean everyone who takes part in design; a user, a computer expert, or some other expert. This is potentially confusing, however, because we often talk about professional designers, such as computer experts, as designers too. I hope that it is clear to the reader when I use which meaning of the word.

[52] In the UTOPIA project, it proved valuable not only to look at the way page makeup was done with the latest generation of technology but also how it was done with the technologies of earlier generations.

[53] See Mathiassen, op. cit. (note 48) or Andersen, N. E., Kensing, F., Lassen, M., Lundin, J., Mathiassen, L., Munk-Madsen, A., & Sørgaard, P. (1990). *Professional*

system development: Experience, ideas, and action. Englewood Cliffs, NJ: Prentice Hall.

[54] According to my discussion of practice, and to avoid confusion about concepts, I find no need to distinguish between what is a design artifact–a suggestion for a technique to be applied– and a principle of organization, nor to distinguish between methods that claim to cover all aspects of design and fragments that cover only a specific activity. For all of these, I hereby use the term method, even though I remind the reader that there is a correspondence between artifacts, techniques, and principles of organization on the one hand and the different aspects of practice on the other.

[55] See, for example, Andersen et al., op. cit. (note 53).

[56] See, for example, Suchman, L., & Wynn, E. (1984). Procedures and problems in the office. *Office: Technology and People, 2,* 133–154.

[57] According to the quotations from Ehn, op. cit. (note 26), this also seems to be a problem with translations of the works of other Marxist writers, such as Israel and Kosik.

[58] See, for example, Fox Keller, E. (1985). *Reflections on gender and science.* New Haven, CT: Yale University Press or Greenbaum, J. (1987). *The head and the heart.* (DAIMI PB-237). Århus: University of Aarhus.

[59] What I have called operationalization here is used in the literature as synonymous to automation.

[60] Leontjew, A. N. (1981a). The problem of activity in psychology. In J. V. Wertsch (Ed.). *The concept of activity in Soviet psychology.* Armonk, NY: Sharpe. (p. 64).

[61] Tikhomirov, O. K. (1981). *The psychological consequences of computation.* In J. V. Wertsch, ibid. (pp. 256-278).

[62] See discussions in Ehn, op. cit. (note 26).

Chapter 3

User Interface Design: The Empirical Cases

User interface design takes place in a number of different activities in the design of computer applications. Decisions made early in the design process, in activities with goals other than user interface design, will constrain the possibilities of user interface design. An example of this is decisions made early regarding the choice of a fourth-generation tool to be applied in the design activity. Not acknowledging this has resulted in design methods that require user interface design to take place as a single isolated activity, late in the process and often conducted by a different group of designers than the rest.[1] In this chapter, I discuss different examples, taken from my empirical cases, of activities where user interface design was taking place. I deal with design activities that pertain to user interface design and not necessarily with those that pertain to the construction of the user interface. My focus is those activities where a major part of the effort is directed toward the investigation or construction of the appearance of the computer application in use. These activities are collective activities, which in turn are parts of the total collective activity that constitutes the **design** of a specific computer application and its environment.

In Chapter 2, I discussed user interface design from a theoretical point of view. It is obvious that one doesn't start to work on a theoretical approach such as the human activity approach without good reasons. The best reason for me was that I perceived there to be a discrepancy between my practical experiences with user interface design and the theoretical explanations and methods in the literature–why could I not find explanations and solutions to my empirical problems in the literature? Why did methods prescribe techniques that didn't seem to work from the perspective of the empirical findings?

In this chapter, I present some of my experiences. First, I hope that this presentation helps the readers to better understand my reasons for choosing the theoretical framework. Second, I use the empirical cases as examples in the discussions to be found in the following chapters. The reader perhaps wonders why I chose to present the theoretical approach before its empirical background. This was done because the presentation is not only meant as a detached presentation of the empirical background but also as a demonstration of the use of the human activity framework in the structuring of the discussion of design activities and design practice.

The chapter starts with a discussion of the common properties of the design activities of interest. Following this, six design situations, originating from the UTOPIA, Aarhus Polytechnics, and Xerox PARC projects, are presented. Finally, a short discussion of differences and similarities is given.

Design activities

Common to the projects was that they made use of a prototyping design strategy, where the users took part in constructing and evaluating the prototypes. All the projects viewed the design activity as a learning activity, and they focused not only on design of the user interface but on possible/ necessary changes of general practice as well.[2]

The projects shared a theoretically unfounded idea of making better user interfaces by involving users and by allowing them to try out the user interface in prototypical use situations. In none of the projects did user interface design take place as a single, isolated activity. This means that when I present design activities in the following, I focus on the design of the user interface, although other things were going on at the same time. For example, demonstrating alternatives also meant touching upon change in the organization of work.

The projects, on the other hand, differed in terms of the organizational conditions of the projects: the interests, power, and practices of the involved groups, the resources available for the projects, as well as the groups themselves, professional designers as well as users. The domains of use for the artifacts also differed, as did the way the artifacts were intended to support the communicative and the instrumental sides of human work and the way they were to be used in individual or collective work.

Finally, the six examples employed different design methods, partially due to different objectives of the activities: to discuss alternatives, to construct specific aspects of the user interface, and so on. It is important for the following discussions to find out about the relationship between the methods employed and the possibilities of focusing on different aspects of the user interface.

The UTOPIA project

It was the basic idea in the UTOPIA project that what was designed were tools for competent graphic work:[3]

> The design strategy of the UTOPIA project is based on a *tool perspective*. The computer support is designed as a collection of tools for the skilled worker to use. The tool perspective takes the *work process* as its origin rather than data or information flow. This means: *not* detailed analysis, description and formalization of qualifications *but* development of professional education based on the skills of professionals; *not* information flow analysis and systems description *but* specification of tools.

This means that the artifacts were developed primarily to mediate the actions and operations of individual human beings toward things.[4] The goals were to start with the practice of the graphic workers and to design artifacts that were in line with traditional artifacts. An equally important part of the project was research on organization of the work process, including coordination and communication, to supplement the development of the individual tools.

The conditions of the design activities of the UTOPIA project can be summarized as follows: The project was sponsored by the Nordic Graphics Workers' Union, conducted by graphic workers and researchers with the purpose of providing new technological alternatives for competent graphic workers to use. There was no direct relation to a specific organization of use. Due to the researchers' background the project had access to a wide variety of design methods at different levels, supporting focus on different aspects of the future use activity. However, access to computer equipment was limited by what can be seen as either economic resources or commercially available technology.

In the following sections, I present three design activities from the UTOPIA project.

Mock-up with paper

This design activity took place quite early in the design process, after initial investigations and some unsuccessful experiments with the use of traditional description methods. The purpose was to analyze some possible alternative solutions as to how a newspaper page could be displayed, and worked on, on a screen. This analysis was conducted by graphic workers and researchers together.

The principle behind the mock-up was simple. Using sheets of paper, matchboxes, some particleboard and the like, one builds a workstation with a high-resolution display, a tablet, a mouse, and so on. The process that used this equipment, was one in which page makeup was done simultaneously with the creation of the needed screen images drawn on paper. The graphics worker and the researcher worked together: The graphics worker did the makeup step-by-step. For each step, the corresponding screen image was drawn on paper (see Fig. 3.1). The product was a series of snapshots simulating the makeup process, done while using the workstation. This series illustrated aspects such as: What material is shown? What other information is needed? Do we need a menu? and Where should we put it?[5]

Fig. 3.1. Paper-based mock-up.

The researcher took part in the process by pointing out possibilities and limitations of the corresponding real equipment: How much information could be shown on the screen? How could one use the mouse for moving things around on the screen? Where could menus be placed and how were different kinds of menus used? And so on.

Besides experimenting with the screen images, one could also experiment with the interaction devices using mock-ups; the traditional ones such as tablet, and mouse, but it was also possible to invent and simulate various kinds of interaction devices, new ones as well as well-known ones, and try out their use for specific purposes. The following types of questions could then be discussed: Do we need a tablet with a mouse or a stylus? A mouse alone? It was possible to try out various designs of the mouse. Where to place the buttons? How many buttons? This way, it was possible for the graphic workers to take active part in the design process. The method was very cheap as no expensive equipment or time-consuming programming was needed.

New features of the workstation could be developed and added as they were needed. A major advantage of this method was that it did not limit its users to experiments with available equipment. Equipment that just did not happen to be on hand for economic reasons as well as future computer equipment could be simulated. One could play with super high-resolution display screens large enough to show a real-size newspaper page, and so forth. One drawback of this method was that the picture drawing on paper was time and space consuming. A totally new screen image had to be drawn for each snapshot, resulting in a large and complex collection of drawings. Furthermore, aspects related to time were difficult to capture.

When the series of snapshots had been produced, the makeup process could be done over and over again by replaying the series of snapshots. This replaying was quite cumbersome using the drawings. Also, the users were limited to redoing the same work process as initially constructed, unless additional drawings were made. For this reason, the prototype helped illustrate overall principles and let the user try out the limits of the design up to that point. However, it could not be used to find out to what extent the new artifact would help the user build up a repertoire of operations: there was no way of trying out whichever operations would be triggered by the encounter with the material conditions. The prototype could only demonstrate one or more examples of which actions/operations could be used to achieve a certain goal.

As a result of the activity, experiences were gained concerning such issues as the physical possibilities of representing graphics material, for example text and pictures, on a computer display. It was possible to deal with the object-directed aspects and the handling aspects in two ways, which was helpful but not sufficient in design. By going through the simulation, the graphics workers could find out to what extent their former practice was applicable to the new artifact, thus bringing attention to this. Also, it was possible to deal with the static parts of the user interface: how the page could be displayed on the screen, and so on. To go further, more advanced design methods were needed.

Mock-up with color slides

The color slide mock-ups were the immediate results of this need. As the project came to focus on details, also of the user interface, mock-ups that were more realistic replicas of computer equipment were needed, especially to focus on the physical aspects.

The principles of this mock-up were the same as those of the mock-up with paper, but the method had been improved by using a camera and a slide projector.

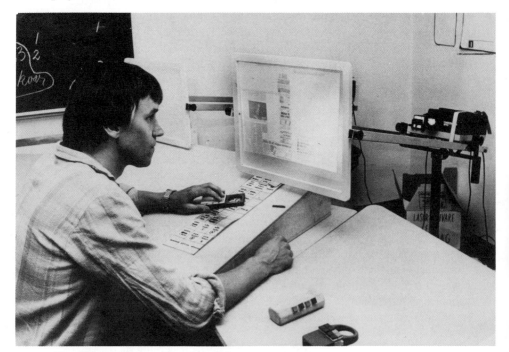

Fig. 3.2. Mock-up with color slides.

The creation process was basically the same, but the drawing of screen images was replaced by snapshots on color slides (see Fig. 3.2). This made the production process much more efficient, as parts of the screen image and other material could be re-used both when progressing in the makeup process and when creating alternatives. However, what was really gained compared to the mock-up with paper showed up when replaying the snapshots. A workstation with back-screen projection instead of display screens, equipped with a tablet, mouse, and so forth, was built. Here, the graphics worker could sit down and redo the work process. It was still possible only to replay the sequences as they were initially constructed. But, as alternatives were easily constructed and the sequences easily replayed, it was possible to let a number of graphics workers try out alternative work processes using the prototype. This way, it was possible to focus on their need to change practice, especially actions/operations, when applying the future application and on their evaluation of the prospects of such a change.

Because this equipment resembled the real computer equipment, it was possible to conduct experiments on the physical aspects of the user interface and to try out, for example, workstations for work when seated and when standing. This meant improved possibilities for examining more details about the static parts of the handling and object-directed aspects and finding out which were the different objects to be handled and to especially consider normal situations. The different paths of the simulation sequence were still limited. What was still more difficult to try out was time-dependent features such as dragging: how to drag a text across the screen—is it necessary/realistic to be able to read the text while dragging?

Graphic workstations

There were, as mentioned, still other important aspects of the computer application for page makeup that could not be explored using mock-ups. Some of these concerned the connection between the movements of the pointing device and movements of the cursor, such as the use of a mouse for selection of text or moving (dragging) material, the use of various sorts of positioning aids, such as gridding and gravitation; and also aspects of coping with the difference between the resolution of the screen and of the photo typesetter.

Experiments in relation to these issues were done on a PERQ workstation. The main problem here was that the workstation provided a very restricted prototyping environment, with no specific support for design of page makeup applications. Consequently, each experiment required a major programming effort. I discuss two of these experiments. The first was intended to exploit the possibilities of selecting text, moving it, and placing it on some sort of page ground as operations. It was hoped to answer such questions as: Which way was the best to select text? How was the selection indicated? Could moving be done by entering or pointing at the destination or by fetching and dragging the material? If dragging was chosen, could text be moved as a box, or did we need to be able to read the text during the move? When placing the text, was it possible to place the text in the exact point, or was some sort of gridding or gravitation needed? Which was preferred? This experiment related both to the handling aspects and to object-directed aspects, for example, could the graphics worker place text according to rules for typographical quality, such as aligning with pictures or columns?

The second experiment was directed toward the use of different kinds of menus and different ways of showing and changing status. Fig. 3.3 and 3.4 illustrate two alternative interaction designs. The first (Fig. 3.3) involved menus on the display screen. Changes in type size, column width, and so on, were accomplished by entering numerical values on the keyboard. The second (Fig. 3.4) involved tablet menus together with a kind of ruler that permitted analogous changes in numerical values by means of the buttons on the mouse.

In the first of these examples, the menus permanently occupied space on the display screen, which meant that the actual working area was smaller than was the case in the second example, where the menus did not occupy any space on the screen. However, in the first example the screen constantly displayed status information, such as type size and column width, as values. In the second example, this information was only visible when the user changed the values.

This setting allowed for experiments with different features of the handling aspects: use of fixed or pop-up menus, display screen or tablet menus; finding alternatives, such as analogous way of changing status and a digital way (editing of fields containing the status information). Furthermore, it was possible to experiment with the selection sequence of operator and operand(s) and with various kinds of feedback from the computer.

The physical as well as the handling aspects were different in the two examples. In the first, where screen menus were applied, the graphics worker could, physically, concentrate on the display screen, whereas in the second, where tablet menus were used, it was necessary to alternately look at the screen and then at the tablet.[6]

The graphics workers participated in the design of the experiments and were the ones to try out the prototypes. This way, they could try out the user interface in a prototypical setting. These experiences resulted in changes of the prototypes and also in a better understanding of what were the possibilities for alternatives, undo facilities, and the limitations, for example concerning the screen resolution of computers. The mere fact that the graphics workers had used a computer made simulation experiments with the mock-up much more realistic to them because they could more easily imagine how it was to move something on the screen, which was not really done in the simulation situation.

The major drawback of the prototyping, as described here, was the lack of a suitable prototyping environment. Thus, the experiments were very restricted and it was, at times, difficult for the graphics workers to relate the prototypes and the use of them to real-life makeup work. Better prototyping environments would definitely have made it easier to make the prototypes look more realistic even though the aspects to be tried out would be the same.

Fig. 3.3. A prototype with screen menus.

General observations

Each of the design methods contributed to the common understanding of *how* page makeup could and should be conducted when applying a computer-based artifact, including requirements for and possibilities of a user interface of a page makeup application. The prototypes supplemented each other by drawing the graphics workers' attention to various possibilities and constraints of the application, including the user interface. In this process, the graphics workers started to use the prototypes based on their previous practice and on mutual learning processes, preceding the design and evaluation of the prototypes. A series of steps was taken in which new breakdowns were encountered and evaluated, and eventually the prototype was changed or an alternative rejected. Through the design methods, very concrete prototypes of different aspects of the future tools' use were established. These prototypes allowed for the evaluation of the user interface through the skilled workers' hands-on experiences.

Fig. 3.4. A prototype with tablet menus.

The concrete results of this design process are discussed by Sundblad and others.[7] The project saw the design of user interfaces as something done as integrated with the design of **use models,**[8] which is the main activity when developing computer applications together with competent users.

"Use models are based on the traditional concepts of the domain, but enhanced with concepts necessary to understand new possibilities and restrictions imposed by computer technology. Such models are useful as means to support design of both functionality and user interface. In education they support activities aiming at creation of conceptual competence. In use they support the user by making it possible to filter away technical distortion, i. e., to focus the awareness on the materials and products."[9]

Some results point at parts of the user interface that we did differently than more traditional design of user interfaces for page makeup systems:

1. To assess a page when the page cannot be shown in its full size requires a scale of a (very) limited number of distinct reduction/magnification sizes.

2. Body text must be at least 18 pixels high (Hp) to be readable. Text must be displayed in reduced sizes as gray scale patterns, not as algorithmic reductions of the text.

3. Placing an article on the page ground can be done by a new kind of tool, the ruler, a way of letting the text float into the empty space on the page under direct control of the user.[10]

The Aarhus Polytechnics

In the Aarhus Polytechnics case, the design group consisted of all the women working in the mail filing office, a number of selected caseworkers from different parts of the organization, a social scientist, and three computer scientists. The project was supervised by a technology committee, which, according to the technology agreement, was a local extension of the central agreement between the office workers' union (HK) and the institutions of the Danish state.[11] This agreement made use of a consensus strategy, where the technology committee had to aim at reaching an agreement, and only in case of failure would real negotiations between the parties come into play.

From the beginning, the group worked with three different alternatives: a restructuring of the existing paper file without use of computers, a restructuring of the paper file with computer support for retrieval of documents and computer-based mail lists to inform the caseworkers about incoming mail, and a computer-based mail file, with computer-based retrieval and mail lists, where all documents were scanned upon arrival in the office. These alternatives came into being partly as a result of management's wishes and partly as examples from the range of possible solutions that the group developed in the early discussions about needs, wishes, and technical possibilities. In this process, among other activities, the group saw demonstrations of various filing systems, scanners, and other relevant equipment available on the market. The project dealt with support for communication within the group and with support for individual as well as collective activity: A case folder–and with it, a file–is a collective artifact because it makes it possible to collect and coordinate contributions and actions of the different caseworkers who held the case throughout time. It is, however, also an individual artifact because it can be used by the individual caseworker to take actions on the contents of the case in a specific situation.

Here, I discuss the specific prerequisites, contents, and results of two different design activities of this process: a situation where scenarios were used and one where fourth-generation tools were applied.[12]

Scenarios

Scenarios of the use of the three alternative types of files were outlined by the computer and social scientists in order to intensify the discussions and make them more concrete. The scenarios focused on the overall actions to be conducted, their sequence, preconditions, purpose, and results. The intentions were dealt with as well as some operational aspects, especially by focusing on the difference between the old practice of how documents were handled and the need for a new practice in relation to this; on organization of work; and on the physical devices of the computer application. The scenarios consisted of plain text descriptions in which each step in a typical day's work with the new technology was described.

The decision to use the scenarios was made based on the varying interests, language, and focuses of the involved parties, which made the discussions stand still for a long time. Much time in the group was spent discussing if a paper-based file was needed in the future, and if so, how this should be organized. Furthermore, it was a key issue for the women in the filing office whether they needed to use a document scanner or not. Much time was also spent discussing the communication between the caseworkers and the filing office. In the traditional practice, it was up to this office to know the organization well enough to be able to distribute the right information to the right people. This caused the problem that the caseworkers, as a precaution, got much information that they didn't need at the same time as they felt that they lacked other information. The scenarios were intended to break this barrier and presented, in the same language and style, three different technical solutions and work activities around them. Based on these scenarios, it was possible for the participants to talk more freely and to deal with specific details because it became possible for them to separate technical possibilities from needs and wishes, and they got a vocabulary that helped in the discussions and comparison of the suggestions. For example, it became possible for the group to discuss the detailed pros and cons of the suggestion for a computer-based file, whereas before, the women from the filing office had dismissed discussing this, due to their resistance to use of a document scanner.

Example

This example illustrates the use of scenarios in the discussion of "computer-based file or not." The specific issue was whether the qualities of paper could be reproduced on the computer terminal and in which cases the group could see a need to save paper originals. The example also illustrates that the aspects of the user interface were addressed in many ways, directly or indirectly, at this early stage of the design process.

The scenario of the computer-based file reads like this: "In the computer-based file, all 'documents' are stored in the computer. . . . The 'paper mail' must be scanned into the computer in order to be filed. Afterwards it can be distributed via electronic mail."

About the filing office: "The women start their day with the 'opening' of mail. The electronic mail must be removed from a queue, filed, and distributed. The paper-based letters are sorted, and the letters which are to be filed are scanned in and distributed."

About the case work: "When a case is retrieved via the computer, the computer presents information about the case, which compares to the information on the folder of paper-based files. It is possible to search for information in the documents of the case or to select documents for reading."

This description gave rise to, among others, the following remarks in the working group and with management: "The letters often contain drawings and similar original material to be used by case workers. It would be quite irritating to have the letter sent by electronic mail and the drawings, etc., in an envelope."[13] The legal questions of scanning drawings and other official documents were raised. Furthermore, it was discussed whether one could preserve the differences among letters, such as paper color and logos, or whether the letters would all look alike on the screen. Experience showed that the scenarios could be used early in the process to reach a mutual understanding of what the key problems were concerning the user interface. It was possible to focus on problems with the current practice this way, but it was only possible to address issues about future practice in areas about which the participants already had some awareness. For example, the participants in this case had already discovered that the qualities of paper mail (color, etc.) were not present when they prepared texts with their computer equipment.

The next step in the process was to address the user interface issues in more detail for the computer supported file, the solution that the group chose to work with.

Fourth-generation tools

An initial paper-based sequence of screen image simulations was made by some of the computer scientists. Regrettably, the future users did not have enough time to participate directly in this work.[14] The screen images were discussed with the working group: which information was needed about each letter, how it should be structured, how to get from one screen image to another, and so on. On the basis of these discussions, the computer scientists built a prototype by means of a fourth-generation tool. The first versions of this were used in demonstrations as part of the ongoing discussions. As the versions of the prototype got more stable, they were also used in the real use setting: The women in the filing office used the prototype to create mail lists. Programming the prototype required much programming experience because much of what the group wanted, concerning the cursor movements and the like, could not be programmed directly in the fourth-generation tool but had to be programmed in Pascal.

The fourth-generation tool allowed the group to run the prototype on the computer that was also used for other purposes in the office. On the one hand, choosing to use the existing terminals meant restrictions on the user interface; on the other, all future users had easy access to the prototype. The existing terminals would have created severe constraints if the group had decided to pursue the most ambitious solution: the computer-based file. The women wanted to keep the characteristics of paper, the font, logos, and the like that were helpful in distinguishing and retrieving documents of paper, a request that seemed hard to support, especially since it was obvious that there would be a need to be able to handle the documents as text, too (e. g. to do key word search).[15]

The aspects that could be illustrated had to do with how mail lists worked: which information was needed, who was going to enter it, how the information could be presented to the user, and so on. This prototype allowed for experiments with the physical aspects, the handling aspects, and the subject/object-directed aspects of the prototype, but within very restricted frames.

The main conclusion of this process was, that it was difficult to involve the users actively because the programming effort was too big for them to spend time on. The fourth-generation tool used was too limited in the facilities provided. It was possible to focus on all aspects of the user interface, but the physical aspects were particularly difficult to change. The weaknesses of scenarios in general are discussed in Chapter 2, although in this case they served the purpose of getting discussions going quite well.

Xerox PARC: The Smalltalk case

In this example, we look at activities as part of the development of the Smalltalk-80 system. The goal of these activities, was to create some application part of the Smalltalk-80 system rather than, for example, parts to handle virtual memory, scheduling, or other basic primitives. The researchers who did the design had extensive experience as Smalltalk programmers. Some had formal computer science training, some had other kinds of background. They developed the systems for their own use. The design of the Smalltalk-80 system was embedded in an unusually long tradition of both design and use, which can be seen as a strength,while also being very hard to transcend.

The applications were primarily developed to support the individual activity, the instrumental side, but they also included communication and coordination facilities. The Smalltalk-80 system as such played an important role as a constraint on the situation. The researchers could change all the rules of the system if they wanted, but there were obvious advantages, for the possibilities of applying their repertoire of actions and operations in use, to keeping the user interface within certain limits so as to make it as uniform as possible.

The principle of the design practice was to start with an idea of how the parts were to look on the display screen and of other aspects of future use. The next step was to pick the right objects from the system, objects that had some of the needed properties, and modify these objects into what was wanted. The process was very experimental: Start with crude fragments of the wanted user interface, try them out, improve them, try them out again, and so on.

This can be illustrated by an example: Assume that I want to develop a graphic representation of the figures of the financial history example discussed in Chapter 2.[16] I want a user interface where the user can enter the transactions of the financial history (the money spent and received, and the reasons for this) and see a graphic representation of the expenditures (a pie or bar chart) together with a curve of the cash on hand. This graphic representation must be updated after each transaction. I can, of course, start by deciding how I want the expenditures displayed and write some code for this. But I can also browse through the system to look for different representations that are part of the system for other purposes. Perhaps I find a bar chart somewhere. I can try to use this with the values I want displayed. Perhaps this is not really what I want, and I might want to change the layout of how the values are displayed by editing the code, or I might choose a different representation. In the first try, I might want transactions entered just by typing numbers in a field. For this purpose I can use an instance of the class called FillInTheBlank which allows for typing and editing of values. Later on, when I have seen how this works, I might change this because I want to enter the transactions by pointing at numbers instead of typing, or by dragging or pushing the bars in the bar chart. Again, I can browse through the system to pick components that are helpful to me, but I may also need to write some code of my own. This design practice ensures a slow evolution of the user interface, while also making it easy to design user interface parts that are consistent with the rest of the user interface. What cannot be seen from this description is how the physical aspects, with the exception of the look of the screen can be dealt with in design. Due to the possibilities of technical assistance, however it was also possible to experiment with other input devices, although this was, of course, much more complicated than using devices that were already on hand.

Discussion

It is remarkable that the most distinct differences among the three projects relate to organizational oriented issues such as the difference in practices among the involved groups, the connection to a specific use situation, and the available resources.

In the UTOPIA project throughout the design process, but especially in the beginning, there were many differences among the practices of the involved groups. These differences stressed the need for a process of mutual learning. The goals of the project related both to the project as a trade union conducted design project and as a research project, which created some conflicts. In the Aarhus Polytechnics case, there were similar problems of differences among the groups of users and between the users on the one hand and the computer and social scientists on the other, the latter also creating a problem because they were presumed by the users to represent the goals of management. In the Smalltalk case, the learning was different than that in the other cases. It was a long-term socialization into the practice of the group of designers/users. In the other cases, the learning was something that occured as a result of the specific, immediate design activity.

In the Aarhus Polytechnics case, we see the biggest differences from the other two cases in the way that **resources** were distributed among the involved groups. The filing office workers and the caseworkers did not get any relief from their daily work while participating in the design activity.

They also did not have the possibility of bringing in their own consultants or the like. This is an important difference because the project was initiated by management–much **power** was, directly or indirectly, in the hands of management. At the same time, the three projects had important **goals** in common concerning the development of high-quality products for and with the users. Resources were present for this, and the practices of the design groups were developed in this direction.

In the Aarhus Polytechnics case, the project dealt with the development of a computer-based file for that specific organization. The future users were directly involved in a process that was initiated by management. In the UTOPIA case, the project was governed by trade unions to provide alternatives that were intended to be applied at various newspaper plants. The involved users were only representatives of the future users. The Smalltalk case, again, is different by its almost total integration of design and use.

The various conditions for the properties of the user interface are seen in the differences in the connections of the projects to a given technology and in the quality of this technology. The projects focused, to varying extents, on the artifacts to be developed–whether they were mediating instrumental or communicative activity or whether they were artifacts for individual use or collective use–and on different aspects of the user interface. In both the UTOPIA and the Aarhus Polytechnics cases it was important to preserve many of the properties of the objects (the newspaper page/the document) when this was to be worked on through the computer application. There was a need in all the cases to experiment with all three aspects of the user interface, although the applied methods allowed differently for this. It was characteristic that the more details it was necessary to get into, the more inflexible were the design methods in suggesting different types of user interfaces and vice versa. Sketching alternatives were possible in all the cases, but there were different types of alternatives. Also, it seemed to be one thing to create breakdowns in current practice, but another, much more complicated thing to create an idea of the repertoire of actions and operations to be applied in a future use situation. Scenarios and primitive prototypes could be used for the former, but they were not sufficient for the latter. Only the Smalltalk example was one approximating a situation where it was possible to attempt to simulate the future use situation in trying out the prototype. In the other examples, it was only possible to demonstrate some aspects.

In the following chapters, I look into the properties of the user interface and the relationships among these, the design activity, and the design methods applied.

[1] See, for example, Norman, D. A., & Draper, S. W. (Eds.) (1986). *User-centered system design.* Hillsdale, NJ: Lawrence Erlbaum Associates, or the discussions in Chapter 5 of the approaches of Yourdon (Yourdon, E. (1982). *Managing the systems life cycle.* London: Yourdon) and Card, Moran & Newell (Card, S., Moran, T., & Newell, A. (1983). *The psychology of human–computer interaction.* Hillsdale, NJ: Lawrence Erlbaum Associates).

[2] For the Smalltalk-80 case, this goal was not explicit, even though the considerations practically involved this kind of thinking for a specific practice: Smalltalk-80 programming. Examples of the consideration of practice can be found in connection with design of support for programmers to communicate while using the system and of support for coordination of the programming activity.

[3] The UTOPIA project has been presented in the introduction of this book. In Chapters 5 and 6, I examine the impacts of the tools perspective on the user interface and on design. This quotation is taken from Bødker, S., Ehn, P., Kammersgaard, J., Kyng, M., & Sundblad, Y. (1987). A Utopian experience. In G. Bjerknes, P. Ehn, & M. Kyng (Eds.) . *Computers and democracy: A Scandinavian challenge* (pp. 251–278). Aldershot, UK: Avebury. The tool perspective is outlined in Ehn, P., & Kyng, M. (1984). A tool perspective on design of interactive computer support for skilled workers. In M. Sääksjärvi (Ed.), *Proceedings from the Seventh Scandinavian Research Seminar on Systemeering* (pp. 211–242). Helsinki: Helsinki Business School.

[4] This does not mean that the collective level was not considered in design, only that the parts of the project in focus here did not aim at producing artifacts for this level.

[5] In the Xerox STAR project, the painting program MARK-UP was used in a similar way to draw sketches of the screen images. According to W. Newman (EuroGraphics 84), STAR would never have come into being without MARK-UP.

[6] Ehn, P., Eriksson, B., Eriksson, M., Frenckner, K., & Sundblad, Y. (1984). *Utformning av datorstödd ombrytning för dagstidningar* [Computer-aided page makeup for newspapers] (UTOPIA Report no. 12). Stockholm: Arbetslivscentrum.

[7] Examples of these discussions can be found in several papers of Yngve Sundblad, Staffan Romberger, and other UTOPIA project members from the Royal Institute of Technology. See, for example, Sundblad, Y. (Ed.) (1987). *Quality and interaction in computer-aided graphic design* (UTOPIA Report No. 15). Stockholm: Arbetslivscentrum or Ehn et al., ibid.

[8] Bødker et al., op. cit. (note 3). See also discussion in Chapter 5.

[9] Ibid. or Ehn & Kyng, op. cit. (note 3).

[10] This is discussed further in Bødker, S. (1989). A human activity approach to user interfaces. *Human–Computer Interaction, 4(3),* 171–195.

[11] An extensive analysis of this agreement and its use, as analyzed from the point of view of the local HK union, can be found in Kristensen, B. H., Bollesen, N., &

Sørensen, O. L. (1986). *Retningslinier for valg af faglige strategier på kontorområdet–et case studie over Århus tekniske Skoles kontorautomatiseringsprojekt* [Guidelines for trade union strategies in the office area: A case study of the office automation project of the Aarhus School of Polytechnics]. Unpublished master's thesis, Department of Computer Science, University of Aarhus.

12 This specific situation is also discussed by Kristensen et al., ibid.

13 Quoted from my own notes from the work in the group.

14 Kristensen et al., op. cit. (note 11).

15 At the same time as the users started to use the prototypes, management got more and more dissatisfied with the work of the group, primarily because the group had chosen not to work on the solution preferred by management: the computer based journal. This resulted in disagreements between the parties concerning the status of the prototype.

16 The result of this process could be the pieces of program presented by Goldberg, A., & Robson, D. (1983). *SMALLTALK-80: The language and its implementation*. Reading, MA: Addison-Wesley, and Goldberg, A. (1984). *SMALLTALK-80: The interactive programming environment*. Reading, MA: Addison-Wesley. However, the described process is purely hypothetical.

Chapter 4

User Interfaces

A general framework, as presented in Chapter 2, is a first step in the direction of a wider conception of what user interfaces are and which role they play in use of a computer-based artifact. It is, however, more like a new pair of glasses, which can reveal new angles and details to us and thus sharpen our curiosity. This curiosity can make us move in many directions where we can seek answers to different types of questions. Many of these questions have perhaps been asked before, but without satisfactory answers.

In this chapter, I try to use this new pair of glasses–the human activity approach–to discuss different kinds of questions, to which I claim that we can find more satisfactory answers. This does not mean that the framework gives new, better, or complete answers to all our questions about the user interface, and it is only possible to discuss a limited number of questions in a chapter such as this. The discussions in this chapter are prototypical examples of both how we can elaborate on the human activities approach about user interfaces and how we can work with different aspects of the phenomena called user interfaces and human–computer interaction.

Furthermore, it is important to understand what the consequences are of the new framework for more traditional conceptions of these phenomena. Will we have to throw away all existing general recommendations? Or can we make use of them, perhaps differently, with the human activity framework? Many relevant questions can be asked, and I have chosen to discuss a few of these. The choice of questions was influenced by the needs that I found when teaching human–computer interaction and by people around me who challenged me to deal with specific issues. This chapter primarily seeks explanations rather than gives recommendations. Recommendations concluding my discussions are given in Chapter 6.

The basic role of the user interface is to support the user in acting on an object or with a subject through the artifact. This means that the user interface can often better be discussed negatively: When does the user interface prevent the user from carrying out the intended actions and in what ways? How do the different aspects of the user interface support or prevent different actions and operations on a specific subject or object? This type of analysis resembles what Carroll called *ecological analysis*.[1]

This chapter starts with such a discussion, and after this, the following are discussed: What is the relation between the competence of the users and the user interface? How can we discuss and explain differences between two user interfaces? How can the human activity approach be used to discuss various more traditional approaches? How can the widespread notions of natural language interfaces be dealt with, and how can the relationship between the human–computer interaction and language be conceived? What are the relationships to the more technical possibilities of designing the user interface. In design, what are the technical possibilities of influencing the different aspects of the user interface?

The role of the user interface

The user interface influences which objects and subjects we focus our actions on while applying the artifact: the computer as a collection of buttons, the artifact as an object, other objects such as text documents, and so on. A good user interface allows the user to focus on the objects or subjects that the user intends to work with. A bad user interface, on the other hand, perhaps forces the user to focus on other objects and subjects than the intended. Reflections like this can, of course, be used to assess a specific user interface in a specific use activity. However, it is more interesting to be able to talk about the user interface more generally and to even give general design recommendations. The aims of the following sections are to find out how the user interface influences shifts in level of actions: Can we identify more specific kinds of shifts, and can we see the role of the user interface in such shifts?

Shifts of object/subject take place in learning situations as well as in more routine use situations, with the only difference being that breakdowns and creation of new operations are more frequent in learning situations than in routine use. In this section, the idea is just to identify different situations of shifts between actions and operations, which are also shifts between different subjects and objects. When I talk about the real object or subject in the following, I mean the object or subject to which the original intentions are connected. In a breakdown, where the focus shifts, the intentions move to one or more different objects or subjects–the level of action changes. These shifts are caused by various material conditions, some of which are adversely due to the artifact directly: The physical aspects or the handling aspects can prevent the user from being conscious only of the real objects and subjects or the subject/object-directed aspects can prevent the user from performing some parts of the activity toward the subjects/objects as operations. The artifact can also support shifts in a positive way because the same aspects support such shifts.

Derived from the definition of the role of the user interface in use, the aims of a user interface are to support the intended or operationalized shifts in relation to the use activity and to prevent those that are not intended. In the following I distinguish three kinds of situations: Shift of focus between different objects/subjects other than the artifact (and between aspects of these), shift of focus to/from the artifact as an object, and shift of focus with the artifact as object.

I use various realistic toy examples to point out how these shifts take place.

Shift of focus between subjects/objects

The type of shifts that I deal with here are constrained by the subject/object-directed aspects of the user interface.

Modes. The most obvious example of what can prevent an intended shift of focus from one subject/object to another is that the parts of the application focusing on one subject or object are more or less segregated from other parts and focus on other subjects or objects. These can be separate applications, running on the same computer. Also modes, and perhaps inconsistency of style of interaction, effect of commands, different icons, and so forth, can contribute to this segregation. Modeless interaction and integration of the parts of the user interface that particularly support actions and operations toward specific objects, cannot, as such, prevent unintended shifts of object/subject.

I present examples here where the subjects/objects are present only through the artifact. For the use of artifacts toward physically present subjects/objects, the discussion is different because shifts depend on the actual physical presence of these subjects/objects.

Imagine a traditional text editor where $e means *exit* in the text mode but *erase* in the command mode. This is one of the problems with modes: A specific command means something and is issued one way in one mode, but means and works differently in another mode.

The Macintosh and some of the Xerox systems are made to facilitate similar applications of programs with different subjects or objects being applied in the same kind of activity. Modes are avoided and the style of interaction is integrated: All applications look alike when possible, and the same command name position in the menu and activation are used throughout the applications.[2] This way, the artifacts are, to a larger extent, capable of supporting shifts between subjects/objects.

Mistakes. Human beings make mistakes when they deal with a certain object or subject. They issue wrong commands or input or they misunderstand the feedback through the artifact. In short, they get the wrong operations triggered.

Undo facilities are parts of the user interface that alleviate such breakdown situations. Undo facilities help the user avoid doing any harm because of a mistake by making it possible to instantly reverse any operation that the user had just done. The operations on a physically present object, or toward a physically present subject, may delimit the possibilities of retracting or undoing something.

In a funny way, undo support places itself between the subject/object-directed aspects and the handling aspects. On the one hand, doing and undoing is something done to the real object or subject through the artifact, which means that undoing can be part of operations toward subjects or objects–for example a typographer trying out different font sizes for a headline. On the other hand, the need to undo can occur because the user has perceived the feedback from (through) the artifact incorrectly or because the user understands that something could have been undone, only, in the situation the artifact is preventing her from doing so; in both cases, a breakdown can occur whereby the artifact becomes the object to the user.

Shift of focus to/from the artifact as object

The support of the user interface in terms of shifts to focus on the artifacts from some other object or subject should aim at avoiding such shifts. At the same time, if they occur, a shift from the artifact as an object should be facilitated. The aspects of the user interface dealt with here are the handling aspects.

The type of situations that are dealt with here are breakdown situations. Both the breakdowns and the support for reshifting focus are closely related to the kind of education given to the user about handling the computer application. Here are some examples:

Breakdowns due to errors in hardware and software: This kind of breakdown clearly should be avoided, although it is very hard, if not impossible, to avoid. *Error messages, recovery,* and *backup* facilities help handle such situations by making it easier for the user to return to normal activity and to identify the problems. Learning also plays an important role: Knowledge about the construction of the application helps the user understand the problem and maybe avoid or solve it. Error handling ought to be part of the competence of the user, and that error handling should be kept within the domain of use. For instance, text editors often cannot open a document after the occurrence of an error, whereas the document perhaps can be repaired through a bit-oriented editor. However, it seems unreasonable to consider the application of such a bit-oriented editor as part of the natural competence of a text editor.

Help facilities: As mentioned, these can also support the user in returning from a breakdown. But, I do not have in mind here active help facilities[3] because in their attempt to adjust to the behavior of the user, they might very well cause even more breakdowns by changing the material conditions, such as the properties of the artifact for the user. Nor do I have simple syntax help in mind, but rather explanations of how a command is applied and of its effect that can be triggered by the user when needed.

Recurring inappropriateness: I begin with two different examples of recurring inappropriateness. In an operating system, we copy one file to another by means of the command **copy 'newfile'='oldfile'**. For most users, it is impossible to remember on which side of the = to put the 'oldfile' and on which to put the 'newfile'. So, every time a user uses the command, she must concentrate on this question.

Pop-up menus give rise to another example. Imagine a drawing program applying pop-up menus. There is a problem of the menu always popping up in the middle of the area where the user is working because that's where the cursor is located. The user can develop some kind of technique to move the cursor before activating the menu. On the other hand, she must then concentrate on where to place the cursor on the screen. In both cases, her attention is drawn to the menu or to the cursor, either because she can no longer inspect the thing that she is working on or because she has to find some area of the screen of no importance.

Through practical experience the user can, to some extent, learn to avoid these situations. It is not possible to give detailed general guidelines as to how the user interface should look to delimit the number of these kinds of breakdowns. Careful design of all parts of the user interface is important. *Flexible* handling aspects can be part of the answer. Flexibility can mean both that there are more alternative ways for the user to achieve a certain goal (e. g. choose between pop-up menus and fixed menus) and that a user can change the programs to better suit her, what is often called *tailorability*.[4]

However, the latter requires some programming language that, like the rest of the user interface, is rooted in the practice of the users: In many cases, direct manipulation environments, such as HyperCard, seem more promising.[5]

Many other mechanisms of the user interface aim at preventing the artifact from being an object for the actions of the user. The object that a user is working on through the computer application, and even the subject with which she communicates through the application, is most often *not* physically present in the use situation. Through practical experience, the user develops a understanding of what she is working on or whom she is communicating with. The imagined object is just as present to her as any physical object, and the user will consider a bad correspondence between the real object and the representation on the screen, and so forth, as a filter between herself and the real object. The same applies to subjects.

For example, for newspaper page makeup, the representation of the newspaper page is important, that is, facilities must be provided so that the user can see the newspaper page without too much distortion from the artifact. Throughout this chapter, we return to similar examples.

Shift with parts of the artifact as object

Shifts with focus on the artifact occur in breakdown situations where the focus is already on the artifact as an object. They occur as further breakdowns because the computer doesn't behave the way it is expected to or when recovering from a more or less total breakdown back to the computer application. A typical situation is that the user erroneously ends up in a part of the underlying computer system, for example, the operating system, which behaves differently than the rest and which she didn't even know existed. Education is, of course, one way of solving this, but it is rarely a good strategy to require that the user know all the technical details to use an application (I can drive without knowing all parts of the engine of my car). Instead, it can be feasible to delimit parts of the underlying system that the user can get in touch with, for example, by preventing the error messages from deep down in the computer to get through to the user. These types of shifts are supported/caused by the handling aspects of the user interface. Furthermore, they involve the physical aspects because severe errors may involve the physical aspects. A shift to some part of the operating system where the mouse doesn't work or to a layer where the screen image looks totally different are examples of this.

What we have seen in this section are examples of different types of potential shifts caused by different aspects of the user interface. To a certain extent, it is possible to relate each type of shift to a certain aspect of the user interface, even though we have also seen examples where more aspects are involved. Furthermore, we need to know the exact situation (to be in a breakdown situation) to fully discuss what happened and why. I go into more details about this issue later in the chapter.

Competence

In the following, I move on in the quest for refining our understanding of the role of the user interface in use. Competence is the primary theme here. Competence is achieved through various types of learning, of which I concentrate on learning through operationalization and conceptualization in practical use of an artifact, that is, learning to deal with a new artifact in a more or less given activity.

From the discussion about learning given in Chapter 2, we see that the use of artifacts where the objects or subjects are physically present will most likely be easier to learn, because the subjects or objects are physically available for inspection. The use of artifacts where the subjects/objects are not physically present is more difficult to learn. Such artifacts will in turn be easier to learn than artifacts where there are no physical subjects/objects outside the artifact. For the latter two categories, a direct graphic display of an object (in the artifact) and a direct interaction style will be easier to learn to handle than a less direct display and interaction style, for example, based on the typing of commands, and so forth. As for many other general statements made in this chapter, those just given must be interpreted in the context of a specific use situation where specific conditions might have more influence and thus overrule this effect. On the other hand, considerations like the ones mentioned can be useful in design.

A user will learn to master a certain artifact through practical use but also through education. Educational material and documentation are important, but I have chosen to refrain from more elaborate examinations of this area.

I look at the relationship between the required competence of the users and the user interface: From an analysis of the user interface can we see what type of competence is required of the user? In which ways can the user interface support or prevent learning? I use the conclusions about learning in Chapter 2 and the ideas about competence as presented by H. Dreyfus and S. Dreyfus[6]

who, in an operational way, presented a framework and some explanations
that can be understood in terms of the human activity approach.

Dreyfus and Dreyfus dealt with competence achieved especially through
reading and practical experience, called *instruction*. They discussed five levels
of competence, which with the concepts of Chapter 2, can be described as
follows:

The **novice** conducts the work process by conscious actions following
rules, also actions toward the artifact. These rules are learned as theory and
applied based on a theoretical competence about the material conditions.
Operations are scarce and very specific. It is often not clear for the novice
what the connection is between the actions and the goals of the total activity.
The activity is consciously planned. Many breakdowns occur.

The **advanced beginner** has developed some set of situation specific
operations that are based on situation specific practical experience, some of
which are directed toward the artifact.

The **competent** user has more general operations and begins to use
abbreviations, that is, to assess as already operationalized the material
conditions and skip operations. Many breakdowns occur because the
competent user often overestimates the generality of operations and applies
these to inappropriate material conditions. The competent user has some
experience in understanding how different planned actions contribute to the
total activity and is able to choose between important and less important
parts of the activity.

The **proficient** user relies on a wide repertoire of operations, masters the
use of the artifact in many types of activities, and masters abbreviation in a
still consciously planned activity. The proficient user normally does not carry
out actions on the artifact.

The **expert** can carry out the activity totally operationalized, so that even
the planning of the implementation is something triggered by the encounter
with the material conditions.

In the following, I use these levels of competence in the discussion of
how user interfaces support the use at different levels of competence, as well
as shifts of levels of competence. Again, this **how** is easier determined
negatively: How do user interfaces prevent use at some level of competence,
as well as shifts between levels? I do not use many of the details of the levels
of Dreyfus and Dreyfus, rather I use the difference between the novice and the
expert and some of the important changes along the road from novice to
expert.

From many practical examples it can be seen that the user interface can
prevent novices from efficient use without supplementing education.
Operating systems with a complex, and often powerful, command syntax are

well-known examples of this.[7] According to the recent discussion, complexity in how things are done can be one explanation for this phenomenon. In the following, we discuss whether the opposite can be the case as well, that is, whether user interfaces can be designed to prevent users from becoming experts, and in particular to prevent users from treating the computer application as an artifact.

Prompts

The first example of user interface elements that specifically support some levels of competence while neglecting others deals with prompting. Often, user interfaces are built to support the novice, meaning that the interface will help her choose the right commands, get the right command or input format, and so on. This can be done in a variety of ways through interaction processes controlled by the computer, for example, through *prompts* to which the user has a very restricted amount of answers, answering *yes* or *no* or a number, or pointing. Or there can be very complex instructions from the computer, such as

? copy

which file from, answer with name followed by cr? oldfile

which file to, answer with name followed by cr? newfile

These and similar prompts help the novice get started, guide her to follow the rules of interacting with the artifact, get the commands right, and so on, but they are inefficient and restricting for more competent users. Many responses are needed to achieve even simple results, and input must be entered in the exact order requested by the computer. This kind of interaction makes it hard for the competent user to keep track of the overall goal.

Furthermore, such prompting can prevent operationalization and especially abbreviation because there is no way of getting around answering all the questions each time, no matter whether the answers are necessary or not. In general, there are many ways out of this. In this situation, to be able to type ahead might help; more advanced solutions would be for users to be able to change the prompts or to choose between different defaults and change this choice as they get more experienced.

Standards and control

According to Dreyfus and Dreyfus, the expert has operationalized the switch between different operations. However, switches occur on the lower levels of competence as well, although they are based on conscious analysis and choice. In general, a user works at a relatively high level of action in familiar situations, whereas she switches to a lower level in new or less frequent situations because she has to use unfamiliar features of the artifact or because she needs more detailed control of the product of her activity. For the novice, there is a big distance between the objects that she focuses her actions on and the real goal or object of the activity.

The following is an example of a shift in an unfamiliar situation: A user is creating a document and applying some kind of editor. For most of the text she applies a standard format, but for a couple of paragraphs she wants a nonstandard format. Depending on the document editor, the standard format is either applied via the computer (e. g. a macro in TEX[8]) or via some set of operations that she does herself (copying a ruler in MacWrite[9] and pasting it in the right place, etc.). Now she gets to the place where she wants to do something special. The questions are what, and how can she achieve this? In some applications, she can only choose another standard format, the application is automated up to the level of formats. This makes it *simple* to use for less competent users, but an *expert* user will often find it too inflexible because she wants to have a more *detailed control* of the formats. In other applications (e. g. MacWrite), formats can be changed more directly. On the other hand, in MacWrite the user must always do all the operations for each paragraph. The user will have to create formats by her own set of operations, they become a kind of cultural techniques, but they cannot be programmed into the application.

As in the previous example, there are solutions to this problem. In the Camex[10] newspaper system, formats can be built, as in MacWrite, and copied without copying the text.

Response times

Response time[11] is also something that can cause recurring breakdowns and thus prevent the forming of operations at different levels of competence. For the novice, response times are not very important because novices conduct low-level actions step-by-step without a feel for the overall goal. For the higher levels it is different: Take a log-in procedure of some computer:[12]

xx login: Bodker   *The user answers, time passes*
UNIX system version 3.4 *of Sept. 10, 1985*
                              Time passes

VT100 _ ↓   *The system expects an answer*
                              the user answers

                              Time passes
You have mail
                              Time passes
Read mail now?_no ↓   *The system expects an answer*
                              The user answers

                              Time passes
There is news
                              Time passes

Read news now?_ ↓

This causes breakdowns primarily because the user rapidly learns that there is
no need to think out the answers–the system needs the same answers each
time. Because the system needs these answers to proceed, the user is forced to
be conscious about the computer application. However, the main problem is
that type-ahead is not allowed; in most cases where type-ahead is possible,
the user would easily learn to type the needed information and then wait until
the computer was done and ready to act as the artifact that the user needs.

Conclusions about competence

The previous discussion is elaborated on in the sections to come in this
chapter. The prime lesson is that parts of the user interface that support some
levels of competence might cause breakdowns at others. This does not only
mean that novices cannot make full use of user interfaces designed for
experts, but also that experts cannot make full use of user interfaces designed
for novices.

This means that in design it is necessary to be aware of the competence
that is expected of the future users. Furthermore, education must be designed
for the users so that they can be brought at least to the lowest level of
competence supported by the computer application, and so that they can
make use of the application at all intended levels of competence.

So far I have talked very little about the domain of competence. We can
talk about expertise in a very narrow way, dealing only with the handling of

a specific artifact–with a narrow purpose–or more widely with expertise in page makeup or programming. In the specific situation, we must be aware of which we talk about. The response time example shows that we can become experts at using a specific computer application despite what the designers aimed at–we learn to type ahead and so on to adapt to the application. However, this does not make a good programmer, for example.

Comparison of two computer applications

In this section, I use the human activity approach to compare the user interfaces of two document preparation applications or text editors: MacWrite[13] and Microsoft WORD.[14] The reader who is not familiar with these text editors and the Macintosh standard for user interfaces is referred to a brief description of the two user interfaces given in the Appendix. After a short discussion of the conditions for my analysis, I analyze the levels of competence inherent in the user interfaces, and then I look specifically at the physical aspects, the handling aspects, and the subject/object-directed aspects of the two user interfaces.

In the analysis, I assume that the user is a competent or expert user of the specific Macintosh text editors. This is not the same as being a Macintosh hacker. Even though some of the problems of the text editors can be solved by hackers,[15] these parts of the Macintosh system are fairly inaccessible to ordinary users, and manuals and other descriptions of the text editors do not recommend users to deal with them. A person can become an expert WORD user by using the manuals, learning from other WORD users, and using WORD.

Analysis of features

The type of objects that we work on with the two text editors are text documents (their form and content). There is no direct support for predefining form (e. g. standard letters) although it is possible to make use of predefined rulers and paragraph formats by copying them from other documents. For this reason, the form must be worked on at the same time as or after the content. This is supported by the applications and doesn't cause systematic breakdowns. As there is no checking of language syntax or the like in the programs, it is possible to focus on the subject(s) to whom one is writing, as long as one is only writing text.

As for shifts between the real object and seeing the artifact as an object, the what-you-see-is-what-you-get principle allows the user to work on the document through the text editors. In software/hardware error situations, the

computer closes down, and the user must start all over, that is, there is no
danger of the user ending up in a corner of the software that she doesn't
understand. On the other hand, it is hard for the user to do anything but start
over, no matter how much she understands of the problem. Back-up is left to
the user.

In both applications, user mistakes are alleviated by the possibility of
changing all formats, fonts, and texts back to what they were (if the user
remembers the former properties) and by the possibility of undoing the last
cut/paste command. Undo of format and font changes, more than one step
back, seems to be a valuable improvement in both text editors.

Except for some ways of setting up standard documents by copying and a
glossary that can be used for spelling and format standards, WORD has no
means for tailoring. MacWrite has no glossary and is in general more
limited. I provide several examples of recurring inappropriateness: In
MacWrite, the fixed amount of line spacing is one such example. Good
typography requires more flexibility, such as a 12 point text with 2 extra
points of leading instead of the 12 points with a fixed, unspecified extra
amount of leading (and multiples of this) that one can achieve in MacWrite.

In WORD, some of the prompts eventually prevent operationalization, for
example, the prompt that you get when asking for a footnote (Fig. 4.1):
When working on a text with numbered footnotes, you just want the next
number footnote, and it is very distracting to have to answer *yes* or pressing
the return key each time, when what you are really thinking of is the content
of the footnote.[16]

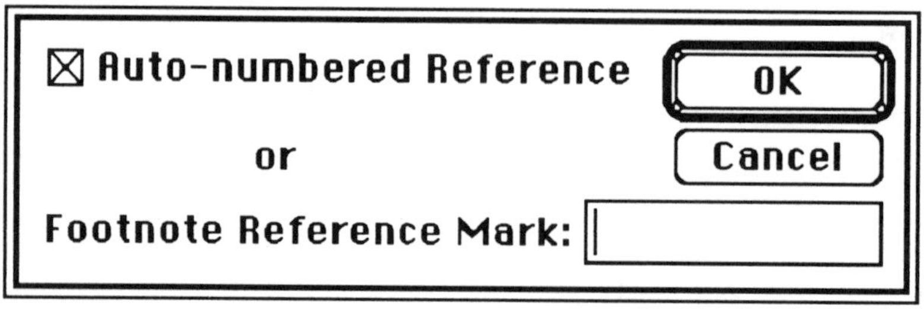

```
┌─────────────────────────────────────────────────┐
│ ┌─────────────────────────────────────────────┐ │
│ │  ⊠ Auto-numbered Reference    (    OK    )  │ │
│ │                                             │ │
│ │            or               ( Cancel )      │ │
│ │                                             │ │
│ │  Footnote Reference Mark: [              ]  │ │
│ └─────────────────────────────────────────────┘ │
└─────────────────────────────────────────────────┘
```

Fig. 4.1. The footnote prompt

Also, it is a problem that the footnote window usually (but not always) acts
like the regular text window. The user often risks getting switched from the
specific footnote to the end of the footnote file. For example, when one runs
a search in the footnote file, the occurrence of the search string is indicated

behind the search prompt (Fig. 4.2), but when the user clicks in the footnote window to start editing, the text scrolls to the bottom of the footnote file (Fig. 4.3) and the selection disappears. This means that the search made can only be used in the footnote window to find out "Yes, there is an occurrence of the text string 'SIS' in the footnote file," and if the user studies the screen image carefully before leaving the search, perhaps she can also approximate where this occurrence is located in the file. It is also not possible to cut out text the way it is done in the main text.

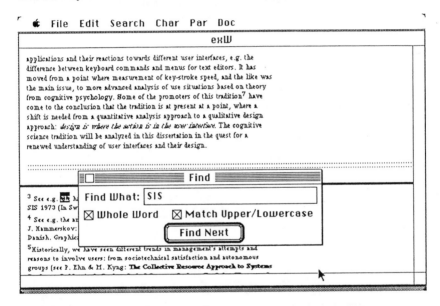

Fig. 4.2. Search in a footnote file, with the search window on the screen. The occurrence of the search string can be seen behind the search window

These are just some of many examples of problems that can be mentioned, but the discussion continues with regards to competence in relation to the two text editors.

Shifts of focus with the artifact as an object are rare, due to the Macintosh treatment of software/hardware errors. However, one type of example is worth mentioning: When in the paragraph menu, wanting to change a measurement and forgetting the units, one would want to go to the edit menu to check the available units. However, this can not be done without canceling the figure and unit that we question, that is, without canceling the new figures and going to a different menu to check the valid units or measurements (Fig. 4.4).

Competence

If we start at the novice level, MacWrite is much easier to get started with[17] because of its direct, quite physical what-you-see-is-what-you-get principles: The icons, rulers, and menus make it easier to survey what can be done with the program and how. WORD is not as direct, and it creates a need for the user to understand the role of the invisible ¶ character and of the figures and measures in the various form sheets. If one does not understand this, mysterious things will happen.

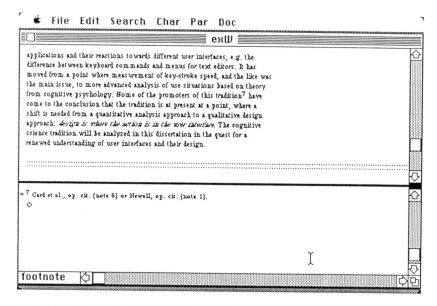

Fig. 4.3. Search in the footnote file, after closing the search window

Through its wide register of ways of issuing the same commands, WORD allows the users to evolve different patterns of operations and, in many cases, use shortcuts for the routine cases. MacWrite is not as flexible, neither in this case, nor when it comes to exploiting the text editors to create good typographical quality.[18] Particularly when it comes to line spacing and to the choice of font sizes, more flexibility is needed.

For both WORD and MacWrite it is relatively easy to become expert in their use, except for the problems discussed in the previous section. WORD, however, has more to offer a skilled secretary, professional word processor, or typographer who is, or wants to be, an expert document designer.

Furthermore, MacWrite is obviously designed to support less skilled document designers and is an example demonstrating that when such designers want to develop their competence, what-you-see-is-what-you-get soon becomes what-you-see-is-all-you-got.

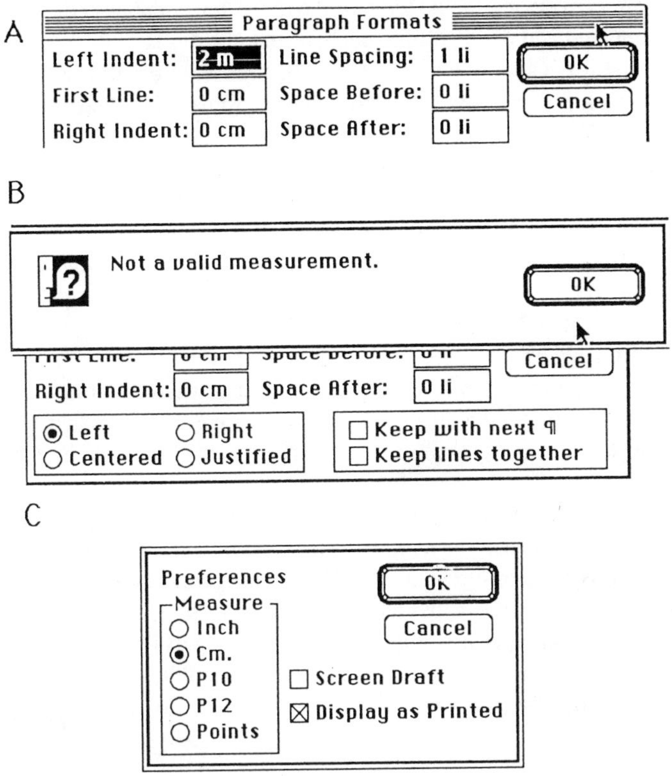

A

Paragraph Formats		
Left Indent: **2 m**	Line Spacing: 1 li	OK
First Line: 0 cm	Space Before: 0 li	Cancel
Right Indent: 0 cm	Space After: 0 li	

B

[?] Not a valid measurement.   OK

First Line: 0 cm   Space Before: 0 li
Right Indent: 0 cm   Space After: 0 li   Cancel

● Left   ○ Right   □ Keep with next ¶
○ Centered ○ Justified   □ Keep lines together

C

Preferences   OK
─ Measure ─
○ Inch   Cancel
● Cm.
○ P10   □ Screen Draft
○ P12   ☒ Display as Printed
○ Points

Fig. 4.4. The user is trying to change a left indentation with 2 m, which is not a valid unit (a). An error message tells her that the unit is wrong (b). To find the valid units, the user needs to go to the preferences menu (c), which means that she has to cancel the change that she is trying to make

Aspects of the user interface

The physical aspects of the two user interfaces are basically the same (the use of the screen and the mouse), although the two editors make different use of the keyboard: In WORD, the arrow keys can be used instead of pointing with the mouse.[19] This doesn't apply in MacWrite. What we see on the screen is in principle the same in the two cases, although MacWrite has some buttons to be pushed (single line spacing, etc.) that WORD doesn't have.

In the previous sections, I discussed some examples where *the handling aspects* are not sufficient. What makes the handling aspects are the filters that are put in between the user and the document: the direct representation of the document on the screen and the scrolling mechanisms, the direct manipulation of the text (selection by dragging the mouse, cutting, pasting, etc.). When the user has used one of the programs for some time, there is no difference between what she sees on the screen and the printed document, except for the distortion caused by the handling aspects. MacWrite has more direct handling aspects than WORD. On the other hand, WORD has more flexible handling aspects: For example, it is possible to change the font size of a word at least three different ways: using the form sheet and the mouse, using Command D typing the font size, or stepping up and down a size at a time using Command < and Command >, respectively.

WORD seems to have better *subject/object-directed aspects* than MacWrite, because it allows for more flexible formatting of the document (i. e. *how* we can do things to the document). In neither the editors is there any direct support for operations toward subjects or objects other than the document.

As a conclusion to this section, it is important to notice that directness in the handling aspects in this case seems to have had consequences for the flexibility in the subject/object-directed aspects and vice versa. This implicates a wider conflict between the what-you-see-is-what-you-get (WYSIWYG) principle and the flexibility needed by the expert document producer. How we can make better use of WYSIWYG for all levels of competence remains to be seen.

Recommendations and frameworks from literature

In this section, I analyze two examples of recommendations for and frameworks of the user interface. These are selected from the literature. The purpose of this analysis is to see if and how we can make use of ideas from the more traditional literature in the human activity approach. Furthermore, such an analysis serves to illustrate how the human activity framework can be used in analysis of approaches from the literature.

I have chosen two quite different articles: the classics by Miller, "Response time in man–computer conversational transactions"[20] and Thesen and Beringer: "Goodness-of-fit in the user–computer interface: A hierarchical control framework related to 'friendliness'."[21] It is not possible to pick two articles from the very extensive literature and claim that they cover the results or the types of thought in the area. However, I think that together with the other articles discussed in this chapter, they are prototypical examples of the kinds of thought found in the literature. I could easily have chosen other examples that would have been just as representative.

Response time

In his paper, Miller began with a discussion of the claim that no response from a computer should take longer than 2 seconds. Miller claimed that this is too strong a demand from a psychological perspective, and he tried to identify different categories of psychological needs for response times. He based his discussions on the idea that human activity is *clumping*, that we have a subjective feeling of having completed a totality of activity. After, but not in the middle of, a totality are we willing to accept delays longer than two seconds. The arguments for this clumping is a model of human memory as having a limited short-term memory. This results in observations such as:

> Novices have their short-term memory registers heavily filled with what they are trying to learn; therefore, they are not guides as to what the problem solving user (or other user) will be able to do and wants to do when he is better skilled.

Miller identified 17 different topics of response to human actions. Before we begin to discuss them, we must realize that Miller's recommendations are, of course, adjusted to the technology of the 1960s which makes some of the categories and statements less interesting today. Also, there seems to be a tendency for these types of recommendations to only deal with the best available at the time they are written down. Miller's ideas can be discussed in two complementary ways: How can we explain them with the human activity framework? Is he right? And how can we use them to make the recommendations of this book more concrete? His topics are the following:

1. **Response to control activation**–click of typewriter keys, etc.–delay not more than 0.1 sec.
2. **Response to "System, are you listening?"**–the shorter the better but not more than 3 sec.
3. **Response to "System, can you work for me?"**–routine requests: 2 sec., setting up jobs: 15 sec.
4. **Response to "System do you understand me?"**–this is always an interruption of thoughts: 2-4 sec.
5. **Response to identification**–type in code, show identification–different acceptance depending on the type.
6. **Response to "Here I am, what work should I do next?"**–this is not part of an interactive use of a computer but more of a production planning system, etc.: 5–15 sec.
7. **Response to simple inquiry of listed information**–2 sec.
8. **Response to simple inquiry of status**–7–10 sec.
9. **Response to complex inquiry in tabular form**–4 sec. (but it depends on whether the delay is in the inquiry or after).
10. **Response to request for next page**–less than 1 sec.
11. **Response to "Now run my problem"**–response depending on the user's own problem–after 15 sec., the user is no longer "in the problem solving frame of mind."
12. **Response to delay following keyboard entry vs. lightpen entry of category for inquiry**–user moves faster with lightpen than with keyboard and expects faster response.
13. **Graphic response from lightpen**–0.1 sec.
14. **Response to complex inquiry of graphic form**–2 sec.
15. **Response to graphic manipulation of dynamic models**–e. g., graphic representation of a logical system–hard to estimate.
16. **Response to graphic manipulation in structural design**–depends on what one is doing (in the middle of a totality or after).
17. **Response to "Execute this command into the operational system"**–response to the fact that the system is going to work on it shortly, the actual execution can be done later.

I do not go into a detailed discussion about the underlying psychological framework of Miller; obviously, it is built on a model of the human being as an information processor,[22] which is far from the ideas in Chapter 2. Instead, I turn to the requirements and interpret them on the following basis: In general, actions are the totalities in which we conduct a use activity. We accept delays after each action because we have then completed a totality that we are conscious of. Delays in an action can cause a breakdown. According to this, we can interpret Miller's recommendations in the following way:

Topics 1–5, 10, 12, and 13 have to do with operations that a human being conducts toward the artifact. As the artifact in such situations should not cause breakdowns, they should not cause any noteworthy delay. This fits well with the figures of Miller, except for 3. However, setting up jobs, as Miller calls it, in some situations can be seen as shifting focus to a different object or goal, which can explain why more delay is no problem. However, this was perhaps the best available in 1968.

Topics 1 and 13 deal with the physical aspects of the user interface–how does a user at this level activate the artifact? According to Miller, human beings accept very short delays for this type of actions or operations. Topics 2, 3, 5, and 12 deal with rather general issues of the handling aspects, whereas 4 and 10 are more application specific.

Topics 7, 8, 9, and 14 are examples of response to low-level actions that the user can conduct on a real object through the artifact, and cover the subject/object-directed aspects. The examples are rather application independent in nature. These should, for the nonnovice, be carried out as operations, thus it seems strange to allow as much as 10 seconds of delay (8) compared to the other figures in this category.

Topics 6, 11, 15, 16 and 17 are examples of response to more application specific actions. According to Miller's estimates, these are most often carried out as actions that are not operationalized. According to Chapter 2, it seems uncertain to make that kind of assumption unless the application has been tried out in the use situation. Furthermore, it seems likely that experts will conduct an even higher level of action, where the mentioned actions are operationalized. If we are designing for expert users, we are perhaps not able to accept long response times in this category.

It is not possible, at least not without further empirical studies, to give as specific recommendations as Miller did, based on the human activity approach. What can be said is that the more fundamental operations, in terms of how widely they are applied and how many other operations they are part of, the shorter delay is allowed, if the computer application is to help prevent breakdowns. Miller dealt with operations that are complex in that they are carried out in many steps by the user, and operations that require much computing. For the former, speed becomes less crucial the more we move toward the top, even though experts carry out even the most complicated activity as an operation. For the latter, there is no argument in the human activity approach why, from the users' side, there are any differences between operations carried out by means of simple and by complex computations.

Goodness-of-Fit in the User-Computer Interface

The idea of Thesen and Beringer was that 'friendliness' reflects the design of the software/hardware, the education, and the background of the user at the time of the dialogue. They based their framework on the assumption that both the system and the user could be modeled as interacting control systems with certain expectations about each other's behavior (Fig. 4.5).

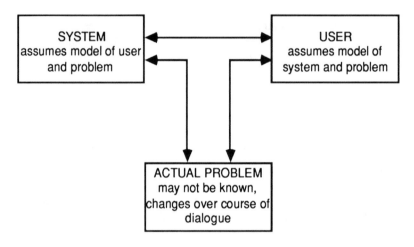

Fig. 4.5 The basic model of human–computer interaction presented by Thesen and Beringer

The authors presented many empirical cases of human beings using computer applications at different levels of action. From this, they constructed a model of the interaction taking place as a hierarchy of what the human activity approach would call operations. This resulted in a conception of the human–computer interaction as Fig. 4.6. This way, the authors identified levels in the system that relate to different action levels of the user. Learning can change the action level, and the action level can change in the cause of the interaction (although the authors gave no explanation as to when and why). They said that we do not know how to build the topmost level today, but that it will not be distinguishable from interpersonal communication. Rather than one user interface supporting different levels of action, what was constructed here was five user interfaces to be applied by the user depending on whether she needs to operate on the level where the computer application supports only the pushing of buttons, where she communicates a vague idea to the computer, and so forth. This way, the application ends up consisting of five machines, all of which can be manipulated by the user to reach a specific goal. As opposed to this, the idea of the human activity approach is that one machine must support various operations at different levels to achieve a specific goal.

The authors dealt with a system as supporting actions at different, specific levels. The problem is, however, that for a specific level of action they aimed at automating all operations up to this level. We can sketch the difference with a text editor example.

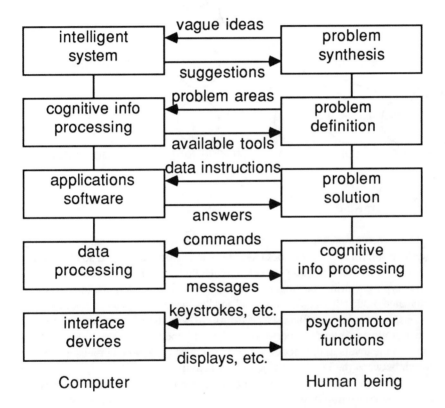

Computer   Human being

Fig. 4.6. Human–computer interaction according to Thesen and Beringer

Let's assume that the user performs text editing as in Fig. 4.7. Depending on which level is convenient to the user, she might try the "write document" machine, where she tells the computer what she wants (e. g. a memo with this and that text). The computer will then come up with a suggestion for form and standard text of such document. The user might also use the "write content" machine or the "change format" machine, where she can enter text or change format, but with the commands at this level. The cut and paste level is where Thesen and Beringer saw commands being exchanged for messages. The Macintosh, as an example, is automated up to this level, but it can also be operated on the bottom level.

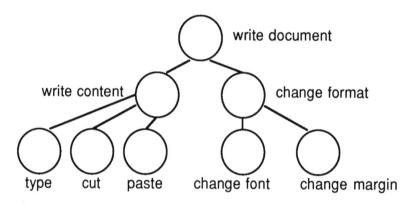

Fig. 4.7 Text editing

With the recommendations of the human activity approach, the same user interface should support **cut** both as action and as operation, and so on. With Thesen and Beringer the user interface should have one specific mode in which typing, cutting, pasting, and so on, can be done as actions; one more automated mode where "write content" and "change format" can be done as actions, but not because the user performs **cut**, and the like as operations. The user always intends to perform one level of operations. How a switch between the levels in the model occurs is not clear (e. g. whether a user can switch between the levels in the same use activity).

Furthermore, Thesen and Beringer obviously conceived human activity as something consisting of instrumental actions and operations at the bottom of the hierarchy and of communicative actions at the top. As a consequence, we should prefer to interact with both subjects *and* objects through a communication of vague ideas. Using the human activity approach, we can say that although the implementation of one activity is not totally planned in advance but shaped in our encounters with the material world, we have no reason to believe that an automated execution of our vague ideas is any step forward. It is an automation of former human actions and operations by which we cannot exploit the human's capability to trigger the right operation for the right material conditions. We return to the discussion of the problem of the computer communicating after a short conclusion.

Some conclusions about the human activity approach

From the two examples given, we see that the framework of the human activity approach can be used to reveal basic assumptions of different approaches and that it gives ways of focusing on both theoretical and practical problems of different approaches. It has also been demonstrated that earlier empirical results can be used to support our theoretical explanations on the one hand and that the theory can be made more concrete by reflecting on empirical results on the other.

Communication partners and human–computer interaction

In this book, I have chosen to use the phrase **human–computer interaction** when I talk about what goes on between a human being and a computer application in use. Many authors prefer words such as **communication** and **dialogue**. They are all borrowed from the language that we use when we talk about interpersonal activity. From a human activity approach, we must claim that interpersonal relations and human relations to objects are two different domains, and it makes more sense to talk about human operation of a computer application than of human computer interaction or communication. In this section, we discuss the consequences of this separation into different domains for the prospects of natural language interfaces.

For many authors, the goal is to be able to consider human–computer interaction as communication, that is, as something that ideally has the same properties as interpersonal communication. Many discussions in the literature aim at analyzing and removing the present limitations on the capabilities of computers.[23] Other authors present analytic or design frameworks where a communicative level of the user interface is important.[24] The common goal of all of these authors is to imitate human communication behavior to make better user interfaces.

In the human activity approach, we have identified two relations between the user, the artifact, and the subject/object: the subject-artifact-object relation and the subject-artifact-subject relation (artifacts used in the processing of material and artifacts used in communication). In both cases, the human being carries out instrumental operations (and actions) toward the artifact (Fig. 4.8).

If we want the computer application to take over human communicative behavior (Fig. 4.9), the relation is reduced to a relation between the subject and an object. This makes the distinction between the handling aspects and the subject/object-directed aspects of the user interface collapse because the computer can only imitate parts of the subject-directed aspects. The

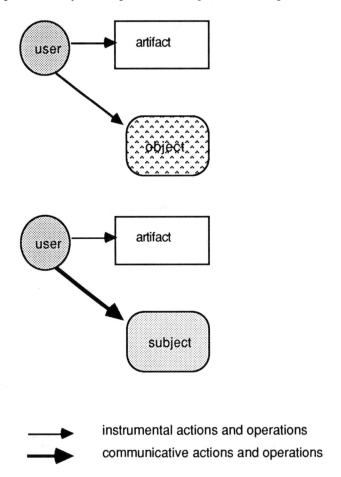

instrumental actions and operations
communicative actions and operations

Fig. 4.8. Two types of mediated human activity

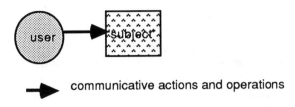

communicative actions and operations

Fig. 4.9. The communication partner reduced to an object

instrumental relation is different and perhaps not as rich as the communicative relation because the behavior of computers is predictable as opposed to that of human being. In other words, we cannot make the computer substitute the human communicative behavior fully, because the computer cannot implement the human triggering of interpretation, which is based on practice. This means that exploiting the properties of the instrumental relation will, in the long run, create better user interfaces than trying to deal with a pseudo-communicative relation.

Our artifacts, materials, and language are triggers of actions and operations in our daily activity. Some of these are communicative and some are instrumental–physical objects can trigger both instrumental and communicative actions and operations and vice versa. Making use of the fact that the human-artifact relation is inherently instrumental means, of course, triggering instrumental operations toward the artifact. Whether the triggers ought to be language signs or signs for physical objects is dependent on the specific use activity but seems to play a minor role for the use of the artifact in many situations. For example, we want a sign for electronic mail on our electronic desktop. Whether this is an icon symbolizing a mailbox or a letter or it reads the word **mail** seems as such to be an almost unimportant question. What can be more important is consistency with the rest of the design, and so on.

The instrumentality also means that we must aim at precision and directness that resembles what human beings encounter in their relation with objects, and not the ambiguity and incompleteness of the encounter with other subjects. From this perspective, the computer application should not try to simulate the behavior of a human being, that is, the triggering of actions and operations based on the actions and operations of the users. For example, the possibilities discussed by Thomas[25] of having the user interface change, keep, broaden, or narrow the topic of the interaction seem to be quite uninteresting. Active help facilities[26] to guide or correct the actions of the users are also examples of computer facilities that are created to try and interpret the actions and operations of the user and the trigger actions that match this interpretation. Practically, such user adaptable facilities mean that just when the user has developed one repertoire of operations to adjust to the computer application, this might change.

The handling aspects of the user interface do, and should, support instrumental operations, whereas the subject/object-directed aspects are, and should be, communicative or instrumental depending on whether we deal with a subject or an object. This does not prevent the use of written or spoken words for command languages or menu entries. Neither does it mean that we must avoid applications that, for example, help the user of a programming language get the syntax right, as long as such help is not enforced by the application and as long as the application does not try to interpret the meaning of the commands.

Tangible as well as less tangible parts of the user interface do, of course, also play a role as triggers (e. g. the keyboard, the mouse, the icons, the documents, the menus, the error messages, etc.). The more familiar these triggers are to the users, the better. Characteristic too, but not unique for computer applications, are that many of the triggers used are communicative and require communicative response; that the computer application is not as clear a sign for its use as more traditional artifacts–functionally very different applications might look very much alike, as opposed to, for example, hammers, drills, and telephones; that the triggers are designed or selected by somebody, the designers. This has made Bøgh Andersen[27], among others, see the computer application as an artifact for communication between the designers and the users, and study the influence of the triggers on the communicative practice of the users–the artifact as signs has influence on the language of the users.

I do not go into more detail about this type of consideration but point out that not only semiotics, as in the work of Bøgh Andersen, but also aesthetics and ergonomics and perhaps even other disciplines have roles to play in these types of considerations. The user interface can be seen as a picture, which triggers interpretations of different kinds, and user interface design can, of course, result in aesthetically appealing, as well as less appealing user interfaces. The same is true with ergonomics. I have stressed the importance of the physical aspects of the user interface, and ergonomics deals exactly with the human adaptation to the shapes and forms of the computer-based artifact in a wider sense.

Summary

In this chapter, we have seen several examples of concrete user interface constructs and their impacts on shift of action level or focus; on operations toward the artifact as well as toward objects and subjects (i. e. of the physical aspects, the handling aspects and the subject/object-directed aspects); on the required competence of the users, and on the learning possibilities. We have seen examples of how specific constructs can influence several, or only one, of the user interface aspects. For example, a concrete dialogue style is part of both the handling aspects and the subject/object-directed aspects.

Furthermore, we have seen several potential trade-offs in user interface design: A user interface designed for experts can be inaccessible for novices and vice versa; flexibility of the subject/object-directed aspects may conflict with the simplicity of the handling aspects.

Given the previous discussion, a phrase such as a **flexible** user interface has been given a richer content:

Flexible physical aspects for a specific application means, for example, that several different input devices can substitute for each other or that the physical devices are adjustable to the individual user or the specific purpose.

Flexible handling aspects means that the artifact can be handled in different ways to achieve the same kind of results depending on the specific situation (e. g., in a text editor to choose standard formats in most situations but also to be able to choose to adjust special paragraphs or documents individually).

Flexible subject/object-directed aspects means to be able to manipulate the specific object or subject differently depending on the specific material conditions but also to be able to do flexible shifts of focus among the different objects and subjects (e. g., through modeless interaction).

We can make similar precisions of other of the well-known buzzwords, for example, **simplicity**:

Simple physical aspects for a specific application means, for example, that the input devices handle easily, that buttons are easily pressed, and so on,

Simple handling aspects means that the artifact can be handled with a few steps of actions or operations and that the components of the user interface give clear impressions of what they are used for and how.

Simple subject/object-directed aspects means to be able to manipulate the specific object or subject in a few steps to obtain the needed effect but also that it is clear with which object or subject the user is in contact.

Other, similar, precisions can be made of the concepts consistency, tailorability, openness, and transparency.

In the next chapter, we discuss user interface design from the perspective of design methods. In Chapter 6, we use the results from this chapter together with those of Chapter 5 to make a series of recommendations for design of the user interface.

[1] See, for example, Carroll, J. (1989b). Taking artifacts seriously. In S. Maass & H. Oberquelle (Eds.), *Software ergonomie '89* (pp. 36–50). Stuttgart: Tentner.

[2] Even though these are the aims of design, the principles sometimes fail to work in the actual cases. Examples of this are discussed later on in this chapter.

[3] See, for example, Fischer, G., Lembke, A., & Schwab, T. (1984). Active help systems. In T. Green, M. Tauber, & G. van der Veer, (Eds.), *Cognitive ergonomics, mind and computer. Proceedings of the Second European Conference on Cognitive Ergonomics, Mind, and Computer* (pp. 116–131). Berlin: Springer Verlag or Fischer, G., Lembke, A., & Schwab, T. (1985). Knowledge-based help systems. In L. Borman & B. Curtis (Eds.) . *Human factors in computing systems* (pp. 161-167). Proceedings, ACM.

[4] See, for example, Trigg, R., Moran, T. P., & Halasz, F. G. (1987). Adaptability and tailorability in NoteCards. In H. C. Bullinger & B. Shackel (Eds.), *Human–computer interaction: INTERACT '87* (pp. 723–728). Amsterdam: Elsevier/North-Holland.

[5] Experiences with HyperCard in a real design setting is reported on in Bødker, S., & Grønbæk, K. (1989). Cooperative prototyping experiments: Users and designers envision a dentist case record system. *Proceedings of the First European Conference on Computer-Supported Cooperative Work, EC-CSCW* (pp. 343–357).

[6] Dreyfus, H., & Dreyfus, S. (1986). *Mind over machine: The power of human intuition and expertise in the era of the computer.* Glasgow: Basil Blackwell.

[7] In my opinion, the UNIX operating system is one example of this.

[8] Knuth, D. E. (1979). *TEX and METAFONT: New directions in typesetting.* Bedford, MA: Digital Press.

[9] MacWrite is the Apple Macintosh standard text editor, for a description, see the Appendix. A more detailed discussion of the editor can be found later in this chapter.

[10] The Camex Breeze system (discussed in Ehn, P., Eriksson, B., Eriksson, M., Frenckner, K., & Sundblad, Y. (1984). *Utformning av datorstödd ombrytning för dagstidningar* [Computer-aided page makeup for newspapers] (UTOPIA Report no. 12). Stockholm: Arbetslivscentrum).

[11] I am grateful to Peter Møller-Nielsen for pointing out this example to me, I return to the issue later in this chapter.

[12] This could very well be a SUN log-in procedure.

[13] MacWrite is the Apple Macintosh standard text editor. The version used here is number 4.5, dated April 4, 1985. I use the Danish version, in the examples also, as no English version has been available to me.

[14] Microsoft WORD version 1.05 dated April 24, 1985. New and very different versions of WORD are now available and some of the problem discussed here have

been solved. I don't think that this makes any difference for my project here as my main purpose is to use the human activity framework in an analysis, not to criticize any specific product.

[15] Examples of this is using other editors to fix files that, due to some error, are no longer accessible in WORD or MacWrite or using the debugger of the Macintosh to write in pieces of hexadecimal code in other error situations.

[16] Of course, this is quite a subjective experience, and from my discussions with Morten Kyng I learned that the footnote problem does not bother left-handed users as much as right-handed users, probably because the former use the mouse with their left hand and have the right hand free for activation of the return key. A right-handed person has to let go of the mouse to do this.

[17] For both MacWrite and WORD there is an extensive manual, but a novice user of MacWrite can furthermore make use of a Guided Tour demonstration program, by which she is taken through all the necessary parts of the use of the program, on-line.

[18] See, for example, Sundblad, Y. (Ed.) (1987). *Quality and interaction in computer-aided graphic design* (UTOPIA Report No. 15). Stockholm: Arbetslivscentrum.

[19] This goes only for the MacPlus and newer versions of the Macintosh.

[20] Miller, R. (1968). Response time in man–computer conversational transactions. *Fall Joint Computer Conference* (pp. 267–277).

[21] Thesen, A., & Beringer, D. (1986). Goodness-of-fit in the user–computer interface: A hierarchical control framework related to "friendliness." *IEEE Transactions on Systems, Man, and Cybernetics, SMC-16(7)*, 158-162.

[22] See also Chapter 5.

[23] See, for example, Thomas, J. C., Jr. (1978). A design-interpretation analysis of natural English with applications to man–computer interaction. *International Journal of Man–Machine Studies 10(6)*, 151–167.

[24] See, for example, Dzida, W. (no date). *The IFIP model for user interfaces* (GMD-F2G2). Bonn: GMD or Thesen & Beringer, op. cit. (note 21).

[25] Thomas, op. cit. (note 23).

[26] Fischer et al., 1984, op. cit. or Fischer et al., 1985, op. cit. (note 3).

[27] Bøgh Andersen, P. (1984). *Edb-teknologi set i medieperspektiv* [Computer technology seen in a media perspective]. The Joint Studies of Humanities and Computer Science, University of Aarhus. Unpublished manuscript.

Chapter 5

Methods for User Interface Design

Traditional user interface design has been bound to conventional technology. The variety of choices has been limited, although it is possible to exploit the technology differently, to apply command languages with more or less complicated structure, and so on.[1] With the recent advent of cheaper and better graphic screens and the like and with changing market conditions, more advanced user interfaces have become something that many designers need to deal with. Thus, access to advanced computer technology has become a challenge to a wide range of designers who often need to change their practice to deal with the new possibilities. Many businesses where user interfaces are designed, apply certain standards to ensure efficiency of the design process, standardization of the products, and so forth. These standards also deal with the traditional technology, and they are often not sufficient to take advantage of the new types of technology.

Design organizations need to change their methods and standards. Designers as individuals, and as members of design teams, need to change their practices in order to deal with the new technology. In this chapter, I discuss which types of design method to look for to cope with the new possibilities. To find the right methods is not an easy task: Most methods do not make their perspective on the user interface or their application domain explicit, meaning that it is difficult to find out what type of user interfaces and computer applications could be the result of applying the method. Furthermore, the methods available come from very different traditions. Some come from psychology and talk about modeling human behavior, some have linguistic roots and deal with the language with which the user and the computer communicate; still others are mainly concerned with how we can technically build the user interfaces and how we can split up the user interface, technically, to achieve this. These fundamentally different approaches make the methods hard to compare.

The aims of this chapter are to reveal the perspective on the user interface of different methods, that is, to present a taxonomy of methods for user interface design. Furthermore, the chapter investigates the possibilities of using different types of existing methods as part of a design approach in the framework of the human activity theory.

Both the taxonomy and the discussions about a new approach to user interface design serve the same purpose: making the theory of this book practically applicable in design. It is not within my practical or theoretical reach to suggest totally new design methods. Thus, the reader must not expect to find here the complete solution to how user interfaces should be designed. Instead I point out possible alternatives to the traditional methods of today. The conclusions of this chapter, together with those of the previous ones, are used in Chapter 6 to make a number of concrete recommendations to be used in user interface design.

A taxonomy of design methods vis-a-vis the user interface

To get to a taxonomy of design methods and their view of the user interface, I begin with some of the key points of the human activity theory. I have chosen to deal with methods, which are primarily prescriptive about the design process, more than with standards which are prescriptive about the product. However, I find that the parts of the taxonomy that deal with the product apply to standards as well.

In the taxonomy, I want to deal both with the general design method and with specific methods for user interface design. Design methods prescribe how various design activities are to take place, how the design work should be organized, how the activities should be conducted, and what artifacts should be used. When we try to assess a future user interface design based on the prescriptions of various methods, we deal with goals and intentions and with the purposes of various prescribed activities in relation to the total activity. Design methods, like artifacts in general, can be applied despite their intentions instead of according to their intentions. Such use cannot be captured by a taxonomy per se but has to be based on empirical investigations. Here, the idea is to reveal the perspective of the method on the user interface and its design, with the purpose of revealing the implicit focus and blindness that the method will cause.

Perspective on the user interface

The aims of this taxonomy are to reveal what types of artifacts and user interfaces are inherent in the application of the method. Following the human activity theory, this means revealing both how the computer application is to function in a future use activity and how design deals with the practice of users. In a taxonomy, it is also important to identify the application domain and goals and purposes of the activities prescribed by the method, because these are fundamental for a comparison of methods. The taxonomy is structured in reverse sequence of the aforementioned areas.

Application domain, goals, objects and purposes

A method carries with it an, often implicit, *application domain* that tells something about which type of organizational change, and of computer application, it is aiming at–the goal or object of the total activity. A method for design of standard accounting applications can be very different from a method for design of innovative one-of-a-kind application for some specific purpose.

A specific activity contributing to the total design activity can be characterized according to its purpose or object, which reflects the goal of the total activity. Design methods, the way they prescribe actions to be taken in different activities, prescribe these purposes, objects, and goals. Obviously, some new computer application is one object of the total design activity, although it is not necessarily the goal of each of the subactivities. Nevertheless, this object is not present in a tangible form throughout the design activity, rather it exists only as different participants' more or less fuzzy visions about the artifact or their reflection about the future use activity. To get to the, eventually, tangible product of the design activity and to communicate about the artifact-to-be and the future use activity, most methods introduce some techniques and artifacts by which to create *materialized visions*. These materialized visions serve the purpose of *constructing* aspects of the future computer application as triggers in *communication*, and they are based on *investigations*, in which visions as well as practical limitations are supposed to be uncovered. These techniques and artifacts can be language-like, or they can be of a more physical character. The goals, purposes, and objects prescribed in a method, as well as the types of materialized visions to be used, have important consequences for how it is possible to handle the user interface (what types of user interfaces to build and how) when applying the method or parts of it.

Means of design, breakdowns and use practice

The means of design, or the different techniques and artifacts suggested by the method, carry with them the perspective of the method, and through their use the users take over the focus and blindness of the method. I am interested in two important parts of this perspective: the role of *use* practice and of *breakdown knowledge* in design.

Methods utilize the role of the practice of use differently. Some take the practice of use as the origin for design, and some aim to start from breakdown knowledge of users or even of designers. Methods can aim differently at dealing with the practice of use: the articulated, the nonarticulated, and the nonarticulable aspects. The different focuses on the aspects of practice and the use of breakdowns, conceptualization, and operationalization have implications for how the method makes use of the practice of the users to enhance communication and in investigation on the one hand and how it includes formalisms, and so on, with which computer applications can be constructed, on the other. The materialized vision can play very different roles: as a prototype to be tried out, a description of the future actions to be read, or a description of the future artifact to be read. Furthermore, in constructing the different materialized visions, the method can make use of more or less complete formalisms, the aims of which are to structure the materialized visions into what will lead to running programs. Methods prescribe both *communicative* and *instrumental* purposes of design activities.

Properties of the product

The distinction between *instrumental* and *communicative* actions and operations is important not only for the purposes of the design activities, but also for the product of design. Is the artifact-to-be looked upon as supporting the instrumental side of human activity, the communicative side, or both? Furthermore, can one distinguish between artifacts for *collective* use, for *individual* use, or both?

I have argued theoretically that a good computer application should not be something that the user operates **on** but something which she operates **through** on other objects or subjects. Not all methods carry this ideal of the product. A characterization of how a method considers the product of the design activity must consider how this product is intended to appear to its user in use: Does the computer application support operationalization, both when it comes to learning how to handle the artifact and to carrying out operations toward the real subject or object through it?

Furthermore, we can distinguish among products of the design activity that are more or less *active* or *passive* externalized artifacts. Methods can attempt to develop applications that aim at getting close to passive externalized artifacts, or they can exploit the computer's capabilities of automating former human operations.

Aspects of the computer application

A return to the distinction between whether the method primarily focuses on practice in use or on breakdown knowledge also leads to the distinction between whether the method when applied will lead designers to start from the *intentional* aspects of the future artifact (the functionality) or from the *operational* aspects (the user interface). Methods focus differently at the various aspects of the user interface: *the physical, the handling*, and *the subject/object-directed*. Furthermore, the way an object or subject is considered in relation to the artifact can differ as discussed in Chapter 2.

As we saw in Chapter 4, aiming to deal with properties of the user interface means aiming to deal with the conditions for *avoidance of and recovery from breakdowns*. However, methods treat design for *competence* differently: Some do not deal with competence at all, whether as a condition for efficient use or as the development of education in relation with the use of the computer application. The conditions for use can be dealt with through such features as help facilities, possibilities for the user to adjust the application to her needs at a given time, and so forth.

Flexibility, simplicity, and consistency are concepts that can characterize the aspects of the user interface. Technically, we can look at how the method aims at exploiting different kinds of technology such as display screens, pointing devices, and the like; the types of dialogue styles desired, and so on.

Design by means of different approaches

In the following four sections, I apply this taxonomy to point out important differences among design approaches in their view of the user interface. I have chosen four different types of approaches that span the spectrum of artifacts for collective and individual work on the one hand, and support for instrumental and communicative actions/operations on the other. Furthermore, the four examples represent important schools or trends in the design of computer applications.

I begin with traditional systems development.[2] I discuss this type of method in general, with an example from Yourdon,[3] as well as discuss some examples of methods aiming specifically at user interface design. Systems approaches in general prescribe design of artifacts for the instrumental side of the collective level, that is, they consider the computer application as a means to coordinate and control work.

Card, Moran, and Newell's approach is a psychologists' alternative to the aforementioned. It is one of the few design methods to come out of cognitive science. With its view of interaction as "a communicative dialogue whose purpose is to accomplish some task,"[4] the approach is an example of a dialogue partners approach. Such an approach deals with the communicative side of individual use, that is, the computer application is intended to be something with which the human being can communicate to pursue some goal.

After discussions of these two well-established methods, I turn to two new approaches that are far less elaborated on. The first deals with computer support for instrumental side of human activity, support for the individual use, that is, the computer application is intended to support the individual human being in her actions and operations toward an object. The example that I deal with is called the *tools approach*, which is a more commonplace name for "artifacts for the instrumental side of individual work". The second approach focuses on the collective level, the communicative side, that is, the computer application is intended to support communication among human beings. In keeping with our everyday language, and with the objective of these approaches, I call it the media approach.

The systems approach

Systems approaches have their historical basis in the idea that the ways of thinking used in computer programming can be used also when dealing with systems consisting of both computer and human components. Human beings, computer components, other machines, and organizational structures can be considered/described by means of similar concepts, and complex components can be decomposed into a number of simpler components, which can in turn be considered/described.

I discuss here two examples of systems approaches: the general method of Yourdon,[5] and a group of methods directed toward user interface design. Because Yourdon's and many other systems approaches are older, we cannot expect them to deal with the new types of user interface technology, such as graphic displays. Instead, the following discussion should be seen as an attempt to investigate whether it is feasible to elaborate on methods of this type in order to handle new possibilities or whether there are some more fundamental problems related to the use of the approaches.

Application domain, goals, objects and purposes

The methods to be discussed deal with the design of computer applications for administrative data processing, typically viewing organizations as hierarchical systems surrounded by political and organizational boundaries. In the world of Yourdon, the system that is going to be changed consists of a number of processes in which data are transformed. The processes can be conducted either by human beings or by computers. No matter which of the two, the processing can be described in the same way by a hierarchical decomposition into subprocesses. When designing new computer applications, it is important to focus on the data flow between such processes. Other of these methods are based not on data flow but for example, on decomposable information precedence relations.[6]

Yourdon characterized his method as follows: (a) it is a structured (top-down) and iterative way of conducting the design activity; (b) meaningful paper models (descriptions) of the future system are built; (c) it emphasizes quality design and better code. Design is seen as description and change of an (organizational) system with both manual and automated processes. The design of computer applications as such becomes a type of side effect.

These methods aim to create a structured activity that will guide professional designers through an investigation of existing organizational structures and of actions applied in use before change. This is intended to lead to a construction of materialized visions of the future computer application (and the changed organizational surroundings) from which the programs can be derived. The suitability of these descriptions for communication purposes is secondary to this.[7]

Means of design, breakdowns, and use practice

Yourdon prescribed the use of data flow diagrams, data dictionaries, data structure diagrams, and structured English.

A **data flow diagram** provides graphic means of modeling the flow of data through a system, the components of which are manual or automated data processes or a mixture of both. A typical system requires several levels of data flow diagrams. Each of the processes can be defined in terms of its own data flow diagram. The **data dictionary** can present a top-down definition of a complex data element. The third major element of structured analysis is the **data structure diagram**. It is applied to describe the logical structure of a data store.

We can take a closer look at where and how user interface design comes in, as described in terms of the human activity framework:

From interviews with the users, the physical data processes and the data flows are identified. Each activity can be described in further detail as a number of activities and actions. In the next step, we go from a description of activities and actions to a description of purposes of the activities/actions only. From here, the system is changed according to the needs, and when establishing the human/machine boundaries, it is discovered which processes are to be carried out by humans and which by the computer. Now the interface between the user and the computer application has been established in terms of which data are being entered into, and extracted from, the computer application.[8] What are designed here are possible subject/object-directed *actions* of the future use. All future actions need to be determined and described at this point. The method does not make any attempts to originate from the concrete use situation, basically because users and computers are dealt with as the same kind of components. For the user, exchange of data with the computer application is not any different than exchange of data with other users.

Interviews with users form the basis for creating data flow diagrams on several levels. In this process, actions and operations are described in the same way, with emphasis on their purpose in relation to data processing.

Because Yourdon's method in the books stops with the design of what type of data processing is done, it is difficult to go into more detail about user interface design.

Several authors have followed a path similar to that of Yourdon, where they use Petri Nets, BNF, and so forth,[9] to describe the user interface in detail. They build upon the assumption that the human–computer interaction can be described/prescribed as a set of states, between which the interaction process moves due to command actions from the user or the computer. This means that this type of method can be used to specify the conditions for low-level actions of use.

Within the software engineering/computer graphics tradition, the so-called User Interface Management Systems (UIMS)[10] have evolved, having close connections to the formal specification methods for user interface design. These formalisms lead to formal specifications of the user interface that can be interpreted by the computer. Often they are combined with a tool box of different basic components of the interface, such as different menu types to be used in the specification.

The common premises for UIMS are: that the user interface of an application can be isolated from and designed after the intentional aspects, the functionality; that the ideal method render all dialogue styles equally accessible; that the method will render complex interfaces more maintainable, and facilitate portability; that the user interface design is inevitably intertwined with its implementation, testing, and evaluation. Thus, UIMS build on the assumption that user interface design prospers by being separated from the rest of the application's design, although it is part of an iterative process where a sequence of materialized visions are constructed and evaluated. Tanner and Buxton[11] raise some critical questions by asking:

• Is there a point where the separation of the user interface and the semantic functionality breaks down? How can semantic feedback, for example, be adequately dealt with in a methodological way?

• Do the systems really push back the complexity barrier and make user interfaces easier to implement, test, and maintain?

• The modules provided in a User Interface Management System will affect User Interface style through the bias of the path of least resistance. How can we exploit this bias to encourage a preferred and appropriate style of interaction?

To sum up, systems approaches, as exemplified by the methods of Yourdon and UIMS, can be characterized by the starting point in breakdown knowledge, which leads to a focus on the functionality of the system, as well as a lack of possibility of involving the users actively in the design activity.

Properties of the product

The aforementioned methods focus on the articulated aspects of the use activity, or rather, they attempt to reduce practice to only articulated aspects. It is sufficient to observe human actions and operations and to get to a number of actions that the users can perform.

Instead of emphasizing important properties of artifacts, the user herself is reduced to an object, one that releases some data when the right button is pushed, that is, when the computer application, through prompts or trailers, tell her to do so. Furthermore, the methods aim at active externalized artifacts, based on the assumption that human actions and operations are reducible to what computers can do.

Aspects of the computer application

The methods basically deal with what kinds of data processing can be (is) done. Except for specifying input and output of a specific data process, which can come from/go to a human being, there are no means of dealing with the user interface.The methods try to make actions and operations explicit the same way after which some of them are automated. The possibilities for the user to later develop new operations are unimportant. Only the security and precision with which the human data process can receive and send data is important.

The UIMS methods allow for focus on details of the previous assessment of user interface design from a systems approach: The user interface design can be done separately from and after the design of the functionality without specific knowledge about the use activity. The user interface is reduced to some physical and some low-level handling aspects to ensure the transmission of data between the subject and the object. With the exception of the computer application, the objects handled are the data being transferred. Together with the type of description formalisms used, this reduces the user to something that has the same type of capabilities as a computer application.

This also means that there is no concern with competence in the method. Neither is there concern with education nor with the determination of competence levels or support for breakdown situations in general. Simplicity of the physical and handling aspects is important because these aspects are used to delimit the predetermined (small number of) ways of doing actions. The formalisms are general, aiming at creating/describing keyboard-dialogue style interfaces (question/answer dialogues).[12] Furthermore, these formalisms do not include any means for discussing screen layout and the like.

A wide range of human factors experiments support systems approaches as they aim at determining the fastest way of transmitting data in specific types of systems.[13] These experiments confirm the concern for the physical aspects of the user interface; the efficiency of different pointing devices for text selection is one result of this type of research.

We can summarize the discussions by giving a brief example: How would a text editor look, designed from a systems approach? Overall, we must emphasize the text flow between various human and computer components. The text is produced or reproduced by these components. If we focus specifically on two of these–the typist and the text editor–the same type of thinking is applied, only at this level they are perhaps passing text strings between them. The subject/object-directed aspects are based on a small set of commands to be performed on the text strings. Each of these commands can be issued in one way or in a smaller set of different, but predetermined, ways (a traditional text editor can be thought of this way). The way of issuing commands provides no way of forgetting the computer application and working on the text. The physical aspects and the handling aspects (the little there are) ensure that the commands are issued the same way each time or at least with very little variety, for example, by providing simple and easily remembered command names or showing clear and easily conceived prompts.

The psychologists' alternative

Within psychology, there is a long tradition of investigating and evaluating the performance of human tasks, especially where a computer is involved. Although methods for this kind of activity have been developed by many researchers,[14] only a few attempts have been made to turn these into design methods. One of these has been made by Card, Moran and Newell,[15] who argued that to be most effective, evaluation methods must be included in design because that is where the choices are made. The authors also said that a post factum evaluation of a computer application is, of course, much easier than an evaluation of an application yet-to-be.

Application domain, goals, objects and purposes

Based on information processing psychology, Card, Moran and Newell claimed the following application domain of their method:

> [W]e are creating a new arena of human action: communication *with* machines rather than operation *of* machines. What the nature of this arena is like we hardly yet know. We must expect the first systems that explore the arena to be fragmentary and uneven.[16]

Basically, they are only interested in the dialogue between one user and one computer application when the latter is applied to accomplish some task.

> The key notion, perhaps, is that the user and the computer engage in a communicative dialogue whose purpose is the accomplishment of some task. It can be termed a dialogue because both the computer and the user have access to the stream of symbols flowing back and forth to accomplish the communication; each can interrupt, query, and correct the communication at various points in the process. All the mechanisms used in this dialogue constitute the interface: the physical devices, such as keyboards and displays, as well as computer's programs for controlling the interaction. [17]

The basic design strategy is based on the following: that a model of the user, based on the tasks to be performed, can lead to a specific design of the computer application.

The design method deals with what Card, Moran and Newell called the performance of the human–computer system (the user interacting with a computer to accomplish a task). Their method starts out with a situation where the structure of the system, that is, the task, the user, and the computer application, is relatively fixed, which means that the intentional aspects of the application are already determined. The method is basically an investigation method, and neither the actual construction of materialized visions nor communication in general plays any role.

Means of design, breakdowns, and use practice

Performance models are designed to predict the performance of the system. Card, Moran, and Newell suggested three kinds of models: experimental, symbolic and data base.

> Experimental models consist of actual human users with actual running programs or physical mock-ups. Such models are *run*, and performance variables are *measured*. Symbolic models are calculational, algebraic, or simulation models. They are represented on paper or in a computer and have no actual human component (although, of course, they model the user). Performance values are obtained by *computation* (by hand or computer). Database models are stores of pre-measured or pre-calculated data. Performance values are obtained simply by *look-up*. Each of these different kinds of performance models has its place in the system design process.[18]

It is a basic assumption that the design process is iterative, that is that it "proceeds in a complex, iterative fashion in which various parts of the design are incrementally generated, evaluated, and integrated."[19] Most of the book consists of presentations of ways of making a special kind of symbolic models, the calculation models, whereas the other kinds are only touched upon.

The three types of calculation models are: GOMS type, the Keystroke-Level, and the Unit-Task-Level. In the GOMS model, the user's cognitive structure consists of four components: a set of **Goals**, a set of **Operators**, a set of **Methods** for achieving the goals, and a set of **Selection rules** for choosing among methods for goals. Card, Moran, and Newell presented the following example of the basic concepts of a GOMS model, a particular model of manuscript editing with the line-oriented POET editor. When the user begins editing she has a top-level goal of the activity:

GOAL: EDIT-MANUSCRIPT.

A user segments the larger activity of editing the manuscript into a sequence of small, discrete modifications, such as to delete a word or to insert a character. Although it is often possible to predict the user's actual segmentation of the activity into parts from the way the instructions are expressed on the manuscript, the user decides which parts or actions. The term **unit task** is used to denote these user-defined actions.

> GOAL: EDIT-MANUSCRIPT
> - GOAL: EDIT-UNIT-TASK *repeat until no more unit*
> *tasks.*

GOAL: EDIT-UNIT-TASK is a subgoal of GOAL: EDIT-MANUSCRIPT, the subgoal is to be invoked repeatedly until no more unit tasks remain to be done.

In order to edit a unit task, the user must first acquire instructions from the manuscript and then do what is necessary to accomplish them:

> GOAL: EDIT-UNIT-TASK
> - GOAL: ACQUIRE-UNIT-TASK
> - GOAL: EXECUTE-UNIT-TASK.

Each subgoal will evoke appropriate operations.

A reasonable explanation as to how they are able to handle goals and operations at the same time seems to be that they consider routine operations as something that can be dealt with as breakdown knowledge, that is, they do not distinguish between actions and operations.

The GOMS model construction may start with a task analysis, and it may involve such things as observation of human–computer systems and simulation of user behavior. The Keystroke-Level and the Unit-Task-Level models pertain to user performance of specific levels in the GOMS model. The Keystroke-Level model has been developed especially through comparative studies of text editors done by Roberts. Roberts and Moran[20] pointed out that the method works only when performance and errors can be measured by an objective set of parameters and that the evaluation presupposes a running implementation of the application. They suggested that designers use some of the parameters for comparison during design. This presupposed that a number of similar applications had been measured. Furthermore, this kind of measurement can only be done for applications where possible error situations can easily be identified and where errors can be handled as routine operations. The type of parameters that Roberts and others[21] think about, deals with efficiency of data exchange between the human and the computer.

Only evaluation of actual computer applications and estimation of the performance based on specific (predetermined) characteristics of the applications are included in the method, not, for example, how one gets from a performance model *to* a running computer application. It is likely that the evaluation methods of the approach are useful in connection with prototypes, but this issue plays a very peripheral role in the literature about the approach. Based only on calculation models, this kind of approach removes the possibility of the user getting hands-on experiences; we hardly deal with an experimental strategy any longer, but a strategy where the user interface can be obtained from a stepwise description of the user's task. Although the theoretical background of this method is very different than that of the traditional systems descriptions, the result is very much the same.

The method claims to start from the specific activity to be performed by means of the computer application. On the other hand, it is clearly the designers who are to make the task analysis (the investigation). The method gives no hints as to how this is done, except that observation of the users' present work seems to be in line with the method. Existing patterns of communication and coordination are not dealt with, due to the focus on one user–one computer. It is not an explicit goal of the method to treat existing repertoires of operations directly, but it is possible to include observations of traditional work activity in design.

The users are not supposed to contribute to the construction of models, and the models are not used in communication in the traditional sense. Rather, users are being modeled and, if prototypes are created, observed. The performance models start from frameworks such as GOMS. They are application independent concepts arising from the design method. The evaluation criteria have to do with performance; not with implementability, and so forth.

From the previous discussion, we can clearly see that Card, Moran and Newell took a designer's rather than a use perspective in their consideration of practice. However, it is the perspective of an evaluator, focusing on how to view human beings, rather than the perspective of a computer specialist, focusing on how to view computers.

Properties of the product

The method deals only with individual use. The user uses the computer application to achieve some task, such as creating a text. The computer application is seen as mediating the instrumental side. However, what goes on between the user and the computer is seen as communication between two components that both have access to a stream of symbols, that is, the handling aspects of the user interface are made communicative.[22] This is the reason why I label this type of approach the dialogue partners approach. The method does not contain any specific goals for automating former human operations, and overall it is does not specify what type of product it aims at.

Aspects of the computer application

The authors of the method recognized a need for operations and they admitted that their method could not handle such: " 'automatic behavior' (operations) could imply use of a structurally different process than cognitive skill behavior . . . . This is simply another place where our simplified Model Human Processor does not yet reflect some important psychological issues, and we do not pursue it further here."[23]

Basically, the method can deal only with activities where there are no object-directed *operations* and where the object-directed *actions* are determined beforehand. Operations toward the artifact (which are really not distinguishable from actions) are determined once and for all, which means that competence and learning cannot be dealt with. However the authors refused to see this as an important problem: All the important cognitive aspects of a human being's use of a computer application can be explicitly described.

Again, we can use a text editor as our example: The typical text editor would approach some kind of natural language interaction style,[24] for example, a language with a limited vocabulary and syntax. The subject/object-directed aspects are rather nonexistent except for the fixed set of actions available to the user. The handling aspects will include such support as spelling correction but also ways of guessing the intentions of the user and acting accordingly. Flexibility of the user interface can be achieved in this way, although this type of adjusting to the needs of the users could easily cause unpredictability, for example, what the user does as an operation at one point of time might not work at another. The inherently instrumental handling aspects are turned into communication this way–the subject is supposed to feel that she communicates with another subject to get this to do something on the text, or that she communicates with the text. The object-directed aspects exist only indirectly through the handling aspects, the relationship between the user and the text is always hidden in the communication with the dialogue partner, but the user is to feel the relationship with the text through communication. Flexibility in applying a repertoire of operations, toward the artifact or toward the object, is not dealt with by the method.

We see that although the dialogue partners approach takes a step toward understanding the human performance of tasks (human activity) and the psychological background of this, the approach still represents quite an outside-in view of what goes on in a specific activity. Card, Moran, and Newell allow users of their method to focus on the articulated and nonarticulated aspects (as seen from an observer) of human practice.

Furthermore, the approach is rather individualistic, and we are unable to treat the collective aspects of human activity (practice is dealt with only as the competence of an individual, etc.).

The establishment–some conclusions

Generally, we can say that a systems approach means a bird's-eye perspective on the organization of use, and a dialogue partners approach means a focus on the relationship between the human being and the artifact. From different points of departure, the two types of methods prescribe that design of user interfaces is done by describing a sequence of (predictable) events or states of the discourse. Taking models of users as the origin of design is fundamental for the two approaches. However, from the perspective of the human activity framework, the basic problem is: not acknowledging repertoires of operations as important to the interaction, nor seeing the actions as changing due to the encounter with material conditions.

The concern of the systems approach for functionality only and its eagerness for automation mean that each action ideally should be realized as one button to push. Attempts to make user interfaces where users can exploit a repertoire of operations (to choose the right button, etc.) conflicts with the idea that all steps can be determined and described beforehand.

The dialogue partners approach assumes that functionality is given beforehand, and that the subject/object-directed aspects support only a fixed set of actions to be employed. Operations toward the artifacts are determined once and for all and are considered as fixed.

Based on the theory, both approaches have three serious problems in their perspective on the user interface:

1. The methods apply an outside-in view of the use activity. They use some formalism, which is not based on the use practice, for this purpose. Both methods start from breakdown knowledge, although the breakdowns causing the awareness are not dealt with by the methods. The descriptions are meant to be read, and the methods can at best be used for observing the nonarticulable aspects of practice.

2. The methods do not deal with changes in the level of actions in use or with competence. Furthermore, the handling aspects are not designed to fulfill the role of making the computer application transparent.

3. The methods aim to automate former human operations.

In Card et al.[25] we see an attempt to combine a dialogue partners approach with a systems approach. This is done by letting efficient transmission of data between the user and the computer be the key issue in the user interface design. This way, it is possible to use the design methods of the dialogue partners approach where the methods of the traditional systems approach stop, where the functionality has been designed, but an efficient transmission of data between the user and the computer needs to be constructed.

In revealing the two methods' perspectives on the user interface, we see that it is not likely to be possible to apply methods based on these types of perspectives in the human activity design approach. Rejecting the systems perspective type means that we have no direct methods for a stepwise derivation of computer programs from the description. In the human activity approach, we must look out for different ways of doing this. Also, I would rather not totally reject using the evaluation methods of Card, Moran, Newell, and Roberts, but so far these have obviously not been developed in the direction of experimental design.

The new approaches

In the following, two new types of approaches to computer application design will be dealt with. They are not general prescriptions of how to do design, like the two preceding methods. Rather, they represent some of the few attempts at design that aim to begin with the practice of the future users and with their work tasks. Due to the uncompleteness of the approaches, I focus on some principles and examples.

The tools approach

The tools approach,[26] as dealt with here, was developed in the UTOPIA project, inspired partly by the work of people who design workstation-based applications[27] and partly by studies of design for traditional crafts.[28] In the UTOPIA project, new technological designs were developed as alternatives to existing technology and to traditional tools. The tools approach is deeply influenced by the way the design of tools has taken place within traditional crafts.[29] The idea is that a new tool is developed as an extension of practice within the application domain.

Presenting the tools approach as a method means that I have to be careful because the approach does not claim any generality and it is not really prescriptive. Therefore, the presentation of the tools approach is formulated as experiences from a specific project and with the idea that other designers can use these experiences to reflect on their own practice.

Application domain, goals, objects, and purposes

When viewing the use of computers from the tools approach, one focuses on the individual use activity as part of a collective work activity. A computer application is seen as providing the user with a toolkit containing tools that, under complete and continuous control of the user, are used to fashion materials into more refined high-quality products. The user is a person who possesses competence rooted in practice of the domain. Consequently, design must be carried out by common efforts of skilled, experienced users and computer professionals. Users possess the competence necessary for a basis for design, but to develop their technical imagination they have to gain insight into technical possibilities as well.[30]

The tools approach primarily deals with communication among users and professional designers. In this communication, the future tools must be tried out in the work process or in a simulation of this.

Means of design, breakdowns, and use practice

According to the tools approach, tacit knowledge relevant to the use of a tool cannot be made explicit and formalized nor will it be. The intention is not to automate parts of the work process but to build computer-based tools that are rooted in the craftsperson's original competence.

An important prerequisite for utilizing computers as tools in a work process is that it is possible for the users to relate the computer-based tools to their competence. To facilitate this the approach has developed what are called **use models**,[31] based on the traditional concepts of the application domain but enhanced with concepts necessary to understand new possibilities and restrictions imposed by computer technology.

Although the tools approach does not claim to have the complete answer as to how to organize the design process, and which methods to apply, it does give some hints:

> For a user to recognize a good tool from a bad one, the tool must be tried out in the work process. In the design process, experiments are needed.

> The experienced end users, the skilled workers, must play an important role in the process. They possess the personal competence that forms the basis for analysis and design.

> The designer has to spend a lot of time trying to gain some insight into the specific work process, not to become a makeup person or the like, but to be able to contribute constructively to the design process.[32]

> Use models and education must be developed as part of design.

According to this approach, a group of people with the necessary profession-oriented, technical, and organizational skills must be brought together from the beginning of a design project, with the purpose of *mutual learning*.

Building up a mutual understanding of the specific work processes of the profession and of the technical possibilities and limitations is the purpose; and discussions, visits to workplaces with different generations of technology, as well as visits to research laboratories and vendors are important activities. For the more design-oriented activities, the use of mock-ups[33] and computer-based prototypes is recommended.

The tools approach stresses the need for hands-on experiences for the users, that is, the need for the users to try out the design suggestions in use. Although tools are not intended to mediate communication in work, it is necessary to deal with the coordination and communication in the collective work activity. For these aspects, the approach utilizes methods for working out descriptions of the work organization. These are wall-graph methods where the symbols are specific symbols from the domain of use and not abstract categories. They are applied in the process not so much as to make a description but rather to make the participants reflect on their practice. Although the concrete descriptions seem to be more accessible for outsiders than more abstract ones, they are still descriptions.

Operation repertoires and their material conditions are dealt with through the mutual learning and through the experimental design.

Properties of the product

In addition to having the objective of designing artifacts for individual, instrumental activity, the tools approach also aims to design passive externalized artifacts that are under the full control of the users. The method aims to create artifacts through which one can operate on objects, that is, the method deals with artifacts for the instrumental side of human activity.

Aspects of the computer application

The method deals explicitly with the possibilities of developing a repertoire of operations. It also considers practice as the basis for design. The physical, the handling, and the object-directed aspects are dealt with throughout the process.[34] The idea is that the tool must be under the complete and continuous control of a competent user. This means that the user interface must support the skilled user in her work after some education, whereas there need not be direct support for the novice user. The method does not directly aim at one specific dialogue style, but it is obvious that the ideas of direct manipulation[35] are well suited for the approach.

We can again look at the text editor example. The approach stresses direct contact between the user and the document: that the document, on the screen, look as similar to the printed document as possible, that the text can be moved, ideally by selecting and dragging the parts away; and that iconic menus are applied by which tools (scissors, glue, etc.) can be selected. The user has the initiative and controls the interaction.

Flexibility, as in possibilities of changing level of action, is stressed by the approach, whereas flexibility to adjust the user interface to individual needs has been discussed but no general recommendations have been given. For the specific case of page makeup and image processing, recommendations have been outlined. Through the design of education, the method deals with what repertoire of operations the user must have to make use of the artifact.

The linguistic approach

Another new–and as a design method even less developed–type of approach is a linguistic offspring. The example presented here comes from Bøgh Andersen.[36] His is only one example of media approaches. Regrettably, most examples are quite analytical, like Oberquelle et al.[37] and Bannon,[38] and do not suggest any prescriptions of how design should be done. The common trend in the approaches is that human beings communicate and they use computers, like many other media, in this communication. Thus, the approaches focus on the relationship between the work processes and communication in organizations.

Application domain, objects, goals, and purposes

The idea is that computer applications serve as media for communication within organizations. Furthermore, the designers/programmers of the application are part of the communication as well. The approach has no explicit formulation of what the application domain is, but some of the examples that are mentioned are electronic mail and operating systems. The method aims to design an artifact for the communicative side of human activity. In the approach, there are no prescriptions of how the design process is to be structured or of the goals and purposes of the individual activities. However, it seems that the analysis of language games and their relation to work processes is important. There are no specific activities where user interface design is to take place.

Means of design, breakdowns, and use practice

The approach gives no direct methods for how the design activity can be carried out, although it generally suggests descriptions based on speechacts. The descriptions deal with speechacts (*actions* in my terms), both with their intentions and operational aspects on the one hand, and with their triggering of interpretation on the other.

It is difficult to give detailed characteristics of the role of practice in design according to the media approach. We can, however, make the following observations: The approach is aware of, and tries to handle, conflicting communication practices of involved groups. Descriptions are to be made as a basis for users' reflection on the computer applications. It is not clear who is to make the descriptions; some third party; the designers who are also one of the groups communicating by means of the application; or the users and designers together. Is it also not clear how this can be done. The method focuses only on the communicative side of practice. What products are created and communicated about in the activity seems to be less important.

Properties of the product

Communication by means of a medium is something that can take place over time, for example, what is sent by the programmer may not be received by a specific user until years later. Computers can only process expressions; the users are the ones who put meaning into expressions. They do that based on their practice. The crucial issue of design is how do users **interpret** the expressions that are communicated through (and eventually changed by) the computer? Furthermore, the difference in practice between the designers and the various groups of users must be dealt with to understand how expressions created by one group of users (e. g. the designers) will be interpreted by other groups. As computers are **active** externalized, they can create new expressions but not new meaning, thus it is important for the users to see when the computer has created a new expression.

Aspects of the computer application

The user interface is dealt with as the relationship between the intentions and the operations of the speechactions. Operations toward the artifact as a thing are not dealt with. The method recognizes the need for operations on the communicative side, that is, the subject-directed aspects of the user interface and the communicative competence are dealt with. For the instrumental side, the approach is less clear, which means that there are no explicit descriptions how to deal with the handling, and the physical aspects of the user interface.

From this approach, a text editor can be viewed in two ways, both as part of a communication between the user and the person who is to receive the document and as part of a communication between the designer and the user. In both cases, we get the result that the text editor must support the user in imagining or knowing the receiver's situation and in applying the proper speechactions in relation to what she wants to achieve. Furthermore, the receiver must be able to know the intentions of the sender from the document. If we use the text editor to write internal documents within an organization, we could imagine that all documents were clearly marked with the type of message they contained: an order, a request, a first draft of a note, and so on, and that the text editor enforced this marking. Furthermore, it is part of the consideration that texts, trailers, and so forth, which are used in the text editor, are chosen by the designer with a certain purpose. The main point of the approach is that the user knows what kind of person is at the other end of the line, that is, that the language used in the communication makes it possible to know the competence, and so on, of the partner in communication.

Toward a new design approach? some conclusions

In this section, I summarize the discussions about the tools and the media approaches, and about perspective on the user interface. I begin a discussion of the implications of these perspectives for the usability in a human activity approach, and relate these to the conclusions made about the more traditional approaches, the systems and the dialogue partners approaches.

The media approach focuses on the collective level on the communicative side. In its perception of the user interface it does not explicitly deal with operations and actions that the user conducts toward the medium as an object. Rather it deals only with operations and actions conducted toward other human beings through the medium, that is, the actions and operations directed toward the receiver of the message. The approach requires passive externalized artifacts, but as an alternative, an explication of what the medium does to expression, as active externalized, and what human beings do through the medium.

The tools approach deals only with artifacts for the instrumental side, the individual level, that is, tools for the actual processing of a product. The users' practice within other areas is dealt with as background for design but is **not** supported by the artifact.

What I am after in the human activity approach is to some extent a combination of the tools and the media approaches to design computer applications that serves both to create specific products and to communicate with other human beings. This way, it is possible to deal with both the collective and the individual levels, as well as with the operations of the user toward the artifact. The question is whether the two perspectives on the user interface, represented by the tools and the media approaches, are combinable.

The custom of the media approach to deal with the designer as one who takes part in the communication is a problem from the tools approach. It is easy to see the data creator (who can be the designer) as part of the communication; but the designer as programmer merely provides the artifacts that make the communication as well as the production possible, that is, the designer provides some of the material conditions for the actual use activity, be these physical or social.[39]

The tools approach treats language aspects of the user interface, not by seeing the user interface as a sign but by focusing on the language use around the computer application in the use models. From the perspective of the media approach, this seems to be too narrow a view of the role of language.

We can recall the main problems with the traditional methods: the use of formal descriptions when dealing with the user interface, the lack of acknowledging the importance of operations in use, and the focus on automation of former human operations. The tools approach operates differently on these points. The media approach is quite open concerning the first problem, although the main emphasis is on analysis of language games if we look only at Bøgh Andersen's approach. Other authors, such as Oberquelle et al.,[40] come from a different tradition where the choice of formal descriptions is more obvious. For the second point, too, we need to distinguish among different media approaches: Bøgh Andersen deals with the design of artifacts, but only with communicative actions and operations. For other approaches, this is less clear. The approaches do not aim at the automation of former human operations, except in some situations where the result of the automation is made explicit.

For both types of approaches, there are reasons to believe that we can move on with a discussion of their use in relation to a human activity design approach, although they do not directly apply together.

The taxonomy: some conclusions

In the next section, I continue the discussion about a possible new design approach along the lines of the human activity theory. However, I first draw some conclusions about the taxonomy.

What I have tried to do regarding the use of the taxonomy is outline examples of the differences among various methods. I have tried to prepare the reader for the following discussion on which means to apply in a human activity design approach. I find that the taxonomy has proved quite useful in focusing on and differentiating among the various aspects of methods that influence, as well as reflect the perspective on the user interface.

We have seen examples of the use of the taxonomy on four different design approaches, each carrying different perspectives on the computer application and the user interface. We have also seen that a prospective human activity design approach will need to cover both design of individual and collective artifacts as well as support for both the instrumental and the communicative sides of human activity.

A human activity approach?

As just outlined, it is problematic to unite the media and the tools approaches and get to the approach that we need according to the theoretical approach. What I try to do here rather than unite the tools and the media approaches, is to expand the tools approach, to enable it to handle the communicative side of human activity as well as the instrumental, and to deal with artifacts for both the collective and the individual activity.

By way of concluding the previous discussions, we can state that it is clear that: A new design approach must take the specific use activity as its origin, that is, the use practice must be the origin for design together with the specific purpose of the use activity. Design can result in a need for changing practice as well as in a new artifact.

It must be possible to design the subject/object-directed, the handling, and the physical aspects of the computer application.

Given the preceding statement, it must be possible to build materialized visions in design that focus on the user interface by allowing the user to try out the computer application in use.

I emphasize here the types of design methods that deal with communication and with construction of materialized visions particularly suited for communication about the user interface, that is, for the examination of triggering of operations toward the artifact as well as the subject/object-directed operations. The reason for this choice is the epistemological reasons for, and problems with, user participation in user interface design. There exists many methods by which programmers can specify their programs, and so forth, but only scarce ideas about how we communicate with users about user interfaces. How these two types of methods can work together is yet another problem I do not deal with. For this as for much of the discussion here, I rely on the competence of the professional designer–that she is able to use examples and principles to change her practice.

The design approach is one where the computer application can be seen as an artifact standing between the user and her object, or as an artifact between the user and the subject with which she communicates, in both cases ideally without being noticed. In the use of an artifact, many different objects and subjects can be involved, which impose different requirements on the interaction and thus on the various aspects of the interface. The approach must cover design of artifacts for both collective and individual use and must look at the collective activity as the origin for design, even though the final artifacts may end up as individual artifacts.

It is important to identify the different objects and subjects that are to be dealt with in the future use activity, and to deal explicitly with actions toward all of these objects and subjects. For all such objects and subjects, the user interface has physical aspects, handling aspects, and subject/object-directed aspects to be developed, that is, for all objects and subjects, the user needs support for operations toward the artifact as well as for operations toward the object or subject.

The ideal is a passive externalized ideal, that is, one that does not aim to automate former human operations, either on the communicative or on the instrumental side, that take control of the artifact away from the user.

The user interface

The user interface is intended to support the users' development of operations toward all the objects and subjects of the activity, as well as shifts among these. Furthermore, it is intended to support the development and use of operations toward the artifact. The handling aspects and the physical aspects together constitute the needed support for operations for all possible real objects or subjects of the use. The conditions for forming operations toward the subject or object at one level might be identical to, or overlap with, the conditions for operations toward the artifact at another level. The functionality depends on the levels of action that are determined in the process of designing the user interface. Thus, the functionality, in this approach, is something that can be seen only in situations of after-design reflection.

In accordance with the change of practice that is a result of the new artifact, the design of education is important. I refer here to the education needed to achieve the level of competence where the user conducts only operations on the artifact in regular use situations, that is the level where the user interface causes no breakdowns due to lack of competence.

Means of design

To elaborate on a new design approach, we need more elaborate suggestions for user interface design methods. In this section I discuss a number of candidates for such.

I start with a rejection of the kinds of methods that consider human activity and computer programs as structurally alike. Furthermore, I suggest that formal specification methods, and so on, are only applied by designers while programming the application. Descriptions that begin with any abstract concepts, such as information flow, are in general problematic because they do not begin with the practice of the users in the concrete use activity.

I turn instead to methods that allow the users to gain hands-on experiences with the artifact-to-be: prototyping methods. Mock-ups, simulation, fourth-generation languages, and exploratory programming can all be considered prototyping in the commonplace meaning of this word, although Floyd,[41] when trying to define the common meaning of the term among software engineers, talked about prototyping in a more narrow sense: "prototyping refers to a well-defined phase in the production process, where a model is produced in advance, exhibiting all the essential features of the final product, for use as test specimen and guide for further production."

Mock-ups

Mock-ups, the way the term is used here, are different kinds of noncomputer-based prototypes. I even see a reason for calling some computer-based prototypes mock-ups, for example, such prototypes that are built only by means of a drawing program. The reasons for applying mock-ups are technical and economical, but one can also enhance imagination through discussions of the ideal user interface that are partly independent of the available technology. For example, in a project like UTOPIA it seemed natural to start from a display screen that in size and resolution resembled a newspaper page.[42] Upon realizing that a solution cannot be implemented with available technology, one can start to discuss how windows and the like can be applied to avoid the problem or begin to find out whether a different kind of screen technology can be purchased. If none of the solutions is satisfactory, one may want to wait another 10 years for a solution. Mock-ups are a way of enhancing imagination.

Fourth-generation tools

The terms *fourth-generation tools* or *application generators* cover a range of computer applications the aims of which are to support users in developing applications for their own use. Typically, these applications can be characterized by the following keywords: *data bases, reports*, and *statistics*. The application domain is office information filing and retrieval. Most fourth-generation languages consist of a data base, an editor for creating forms on the display screen that are to be used when data are entered into the data base; a report generator, by which output lists and statistics can be structured, and a query language, by which queries for the retrieval of data can be constructed.

The fourth-generation tool often imposes constraints on the user interface, as in the Aarhus Polytechnics case, from where we get the following example:[43] In the paper-based file, such things as paper color and texture, logos, and writing style are important in the retrieval process. We had no possibilities of seeing whether these kinds of characteristics were something to work with in the computer-based file.

Fourth-generation tools are meant to be used **by** the future users, that is, the users themselves, without assistance from computer specialists, can design their own screen images, report forms, and so forth. It is the experience from Aarhus Polytechnics that it was easy to get started with the design, but when doing something a little more advanced, very low-level programming[44] was needed. Furthermore, it is fair to say that even though the concepts applied in the fourth-generation tools are application specific, the design must start, **not** from the use activity as such, but from a discussion of what types of documents are available, and so on. In order to take part in these discussions, the users must have some amount of design/programming competence.

Fourth-generation tools share many characteristics with the mock-ups. Furthermore, they allow for trying out aspects of the user interface, such as how it feels to actually select something by moving the cursor. They also impose constraints on how the user interface looks, and force the designers to think more explicitly in terms of what can be done with this specific fourth-generation tool. This means that the fourth-generation tools should be used together with the users but not by them without technical computer assistance.

Traditionally, fourth-generation tools provide a toolbox of components to help build a specific kind of user interface for form-filling style interaction that makes the application domain very specific. Like all types of computer applications, these get more and more advanced, but for most of them, all the prototypes designed in the process should be running computer programs. In turn, the design process is supposed to, step-by-step, lead to a running application.

Exploratory programming

Another example of a prototyping environment is Smalltalk-80.[45] The Smalltalk-80 system is used in the process of reshaping itself to be applied in a certain, more specific domain. This literally illustrates that the purpose of design is the purpose of the future use.

On the one hand, Smalltalk-80 is a very flexible environment that allows the user to experiment with major and minor changes of, for example, the user interface. On the other, the prototyping environment strongly supports a specific practice of the future user. As Smalltalk-80 is designed by its users (and used by designers), this is an example of what kind of design tools and techniques and user interfaces these designers want, or think they want, for themselves:

1. Flexible prototyping with the possibility of changing all parts of the product when needed. Examples and prototypes to work on instead of strictly enforced rules.

2. Programming by copying and changing instead of rewriting, which supports experimental design.

3. A graphics oriented user interface with windows, menus, and a mouse.

Compared to fourth-generation tools, Smalltalk-80 is very different in the way the users can apply the rules of its use. On the one hand, it provides an extreme flexibility in how the user interfaces look. On the other, it relies heavily on the practice of the designers. They must be capable of staying within the limits of the style when needed, and of changing the style when that is needed. Furthermore, it takes some effort to make use of the facilities in Smalltalk-80. These require much more learning and computing practice than fourth-generation tools.

Prototyping

The computer supported design methods discussed here exhibit a potential conflict between accessibility, in terms of computing competence and programming effort needed, and flexibility, both in terms of how the artifacts can be applied and of which user interfaces can be designed. This indicates that to achieve better computer-based prototyping support we must focus on a specific application domain and use practice(s), provide a tool box of basic components that supports different styles of interaction,[46] have access to a variety of interaction devices, and use both mock-ups and more advanced computer-based prototyping methods.

As a final comment, prototypes need not only be simulations in which one user tries out one computer application, they can be a whole play where the users are brought into a world where computer prototypes have certain roles and human beings have others. However, even the best mock-ups or prototypes are only simulations of an encounter with the real world.

Scenarios

In the previous sections, I have discussed formal description methods and prototyping methods and rejected the former. The question is whether we have to give up descriptions all together or whether there exist types of descriptions that apply as part of the human activity approach. Naturally, descriptions can never substitute for the encounter with the material world, that is, description cannot trigger the operations that the encounter with the material will. But we might have a chance of approaching this situation, perhaps as a supplement to some kind of prototyping.

Scenarios are a way of describing computer applications and their use to users. Scenarios can have many different forms, common to which is that they are descriptions. In the Aarhus Polytechnics case scenarios in natural language were applied to sketch different general solutions to the questions regarding a computer application: What text should the user enter to register the mail, how were copies produced, which information could be retrieved by the caseworkers and so forth.? Scenarios can focus on the sequence of actions/operations taken by the user and the feedback from the application.

From the human activity point of view, what is needed is something suited for communication that can help the users start to reflect upon their practice and the way it may change due to a new artifact. Scenarios seem not to be suitable for construction at a detailed level.

Suggestions for new methods

The means of design have strong impacts on the user interface. This goes both for which aspects of the computer application one choose to focus on and for the properties of the future user interface. An implication of this can be that one must either choose to pursue a certain kind of user interface or choose means of design and be aware of what possible types of user interfaces are cut off by the choice.

One recommendation is to choose, in the early stages of design, means of design that is as general as possible when it comes to which kind of user interface to end up with, as well as one that allows beginning with the use practice of the users rather than with breakdown knowledge. Later on, one can choose more specific means, because that makes construction of a materialized vision of the interface easier.

Mock-up, exploratory programming, and fourth-generation methods can be included in a toolbox of design means that the professional designer has access to. They are not to be seen as three different tools that can be applied directly in any given user interface design activity, but as concepts underlying the toolbox. This designer's tool box should then be a set of computer-based and noncomputer-based means, with which the specific design means for a specific design activity can be built.

What I have suggested here is not a method in the traditional sense of a method, a recipe to be followed step-by-step. The reason for this is the relationship between methods and design practice discussed in Chapter 2: Professional design is not done based only on a step-by-step procedure but rather is based on the repertoires of the professional designers, of operations in which different means are applied. In varying ways, the discussions and examples presented here directly aim to present such new means. For these new means to be applied in design practice, designers must try them out and include them in their repertoire of operations.

In Chapter 6, I go into more detail about both the human activity approach and the research to be undertaken to develop this approach. I plan to give designers concrete recommendations for the design of user interfaces, based on the theoretical and practical discussions of this and the previous chapters.

---

[1] See my discussion of Miller, R. (1968). Response time in man–computer conversational transactions. *Fall Joint Computer Conference* (pp. 267–277) in Chapter 4. The theoretical approach of this book is not bound to this new technology and could have been developed without it. However, the new technology has resulted in a greater emphasis on user interfaces, in research as well.

[2] For a theoretical presentation of the systems approach, see Holbæk-Hanssen, E., Håndlykken, P., & Nygaard, K. (1975). *System description and the DELTA language.* Oslo: Norwegian Computing Center. The systems approach is also used by C. W. Churchman but in reference to a different approach which is not covered by the characteristics presented here (Churchman, C. W. (1968). *The systems approach.* New York: Dell).

[3] Yourdon, E. (1982). *Managing the systems life cycle.* London: Yourdon, or DeMarco, T. (1979). *Structured analysis and system specification.* London: Yourdon. See also for example, Andersen, C., Krogh-Jespersen, F., & Petersen, A. (1972). *SYSKON–en bog om konstruktion af datamatiske systemer* (Vols. 1-2) [SYSKON–A book about construction of computer systems]. Odense: G. E. C. Gads Forlag, or Lundeberg, M, Goldkuhl, G., & Nilsson, A. (1978). *Systemering* [Systemeering]. Lund: Studentlitteratur.

[4] Card, S., Moran, T., & Newell, A. (1983). *The psychology of human–computer interaction.* Hillsdale, NJ: Lawrence Erlbaum Associates.

[5] Yourdon, op. cit (note 3).

[6] Lundeberg et al., op. cit. (note 3).

[7] Bødker, S., & Hammerskov, J. (1982). *Grafisk systembeskrivelse* [Graphical systems description] (DAIMI IR-33, IR-34, and IR-35). Århus: University of Aarhus.

[8] I know that Yourdon and his people now teach a method that is a little different from this one, based on the idea of events. It has not been possible for me to get

written material about this, but the ideas seem to resemble those discussed later as methods for user interface design based on a systems ideal.

[9] Oberquelle, H. (1985). *Semi-formal graphic modelling of dialog systems* (Bericht Nr. FBI-HH-B-113/85). Hamburg: Universität Hamburg, FB Informatik. Parnas, D. L. (1969). On the use of transition diagram in the design of a user interface for an interactive computer system. *Proceedings. ACM 24th National Conference* (pp. 378–385). Reisner, P. (1981). Formal grammar and human factors design of an interactive graphics system. *IEEE Transactions on Software Engineering, SE-7*, 229–240. Shneiderman, B. (1982). Multiparty grammars and related features for defining interactive systems. *IEEE Transactions on Systems, Man, and Cybernetics, SMC-12*, 148–154.

[10] Wasserman, A. I. (1979). USE: A methodology for the design and development of interactive information systems. In H.-J. Schneider (Ed.), *Formal models and practical tools for information system design*, (pp. 31–50). Amsterdam: North-Holland, or Wasserman, A. I. (1980). Software tools and the user software engineering project. In W. E. Riddle & R. E. Fairley (Eds.), *Software development tools* (pp. 93–113). Berlin: Springer Verlag.

[11] Tanner, P., & Buxton, W. (1985). Some issues in future User Interface Management System (UIMS) development. In G. Pfaff (Ed.), *User Interface Management Systems* (pp. 67–80). Berlin: Springer Verlag.

[12] In Caspersen, J., Gaardbo, P., Kjær, J., Klötzl, J., Krogh, P.E., & Mathiasen, L. (1985). *Description techniques for interactive systems*. Ålborg Universitetscenter. Unpublished manuscript, a number of this type of technique are presented and discussed in detail.

[13] Shneiderman, B. (1979). Human factors experiments in designing interactive systems. *Computer, December*, 9–19, mentions several experiments. Card, S. K., English, W. K., & Burr, B. J. (1978). Evaluation of a mouse, rate controlled isometric joystick, step keys, and text keys for text selection on a CRT. *Ergonomics 21(8)*, 601–614 compare the speed of different devices for text selection.

[14] For a discussion of different research groups and their methods, see that on psychological research methods in the human use of computers in Borman, L., & Curtis, B. (Eds.) (1985). *Human factors in computing systems*. Proceedings, ACM.

[15] Card et al., 1983, op. cit. (note 4).

[16] Ibid.

[17] Ibid.

[18] Ibid.

[19] Ibid., p. 406.

[20] Card, S., Moran, T., & Newell, A. (1980). The keystroke-level model for user performance time with interactive systems. *Communications of the ACM, 23(7)*,

396–410 and Roberts, T. L., & Moran, T. P. (1983). The evaluation of text editors: Methodology and empirical results. *Communications of the ACM 26(4)*, 265–283.

[21] See various contributions in Borman & Curtis, op. cit. (note 14).

[22] This is not the way I view communication in this book. What in my theoretical approach is a triggering of interpretative operations, by which the communication moves ahead, is in Card, Moran, & Newell's terms a planned exchange of a sequence of information.

[23] Card et al., op. cit. (note 4).

[24] Card et al., op. cit. (note 20), Roberts, op. cit. (note 20) etc. deal with other types of interaction style as well.

[25] Card et al., op. cit. (note 13).

[26] Ehn, P., & Kyng, M. (1984). A tool perspective on design of interactive computer support for skilled workers. In M. Sääksjärvi (Ed.), *Proceedings from the Seventh Scandinavian Research Seminar on Systemeering* (pp. 211–242). Helsinki: Helsinki Business School.

[27] See, for example, Shiel, B. (1983). Power tools for programmers. *Datamation*, *29(2)*, 131-144.

[28] Göranzon, B. (Ed.) (1984). *Datautvecklingens filosofi* [The philosophy of computer development]. Malmö, Sweden: Carlsson & Jönsson.

[29] See, for example, Göranzon, ibid.

[30] See, for example, Bødker, S., Ehn, P., Kammersgaard, J., Kyng, M., & Sundblad, Y. (1987). A Utopian experience. In G. Bjerknes, P. Ehn, & M. Kyng (Eds.). *Computers and democracy: A Scandinavian challenge.*(pp. 251–278). Aldershot, UK: Avebury.

31 For a detailed discussion of use models, see Kammersgaard, J. (1985b). On models and their role in the use of computers. *Preceedings of the Aarhus Conference on Development and Use of Computer-based Systems and Tools* (pp. 241–250). Århus: University of Aarhus.

[32] Bødker et al., op. cit. (note 30).

[33] For a description of mock-ups and the other methods applied by the UTOPIA project see Chapter 3.

[34] For a detailed description, see Chapter 3.

[35] See, for example Shneiderman, B. (1983). Direct manipulation: A step beyond programming languages. *Computer, August,* 57–69.

[36] Bøgh Andersen, P. (1984). *Edb-teknologi set i medieperspektiv* [Computer technology seen in a media perspective]. The Joint Studies of Humanities and Computer Science, University of Aarhus. Unpublished manuscript.

[37] Oberquelle, H., Kupka, I., & Maass, S. (1983). A view of human–machine communication and cooperation. *International Journal of Man–Machine Studies, 19(4),* 309–333.

[38] Bannon, L. (1986). Computer-mediated communication. In D. A. Norman & S. W. Draper (Eds.), *User–centered system design* (pp. 433–452). Hillsdale, NJ: Lawrence Erlbaum Associates.

[39] For a discussion of the role of the user interface as signs in communication, see Chapter 4.

[40] H. Oberquelle et al., op. cit. (note 37).

[41] Floyd, C. (1984). A systematic look at prototyping. In R. Budde, K. Kühlenkamp, L. Mathiassen, & H. Züllighoven (Eds.), *Approaches to prototyping* (pp. 1-18). Berlin: Springer Verlag.

[42] Bødker, S., Ehn, P., Romberger, S., & Sjögren, D. (Eds.) (1985). *Graffiti 7. The UTOPIA project: An alternative in text and images.* Stockholm:Arbetslivcentrum.

[43] See discussion in Chapter 3.

[44] See also Kristensen, B. H., Bollesen, N., & Sørensen, O. L. (1986). *Retningslinier for valg af faglige strategier på kontorområdet–et case studie over Århus tekniske Skoles kontorautomatiseringsprojekt* [Guidelines for trade union strategies in the office area: A case study of the office automation project of the Aarhus School of Polytechnics]. Unpublished master's thesis, Department of Computer Science, University of Aarhus.

[45] Goldberg, A. (1984). *SMALLTALK-80: The interactive programming environment.* Reading, MA: Addison-Wesley, p. 20. This is perhaps a rather unorthodox interpretation of the goals of applying the Smalltalk-80 system.

[46] Smalltalk-80 supports the basic idea of this by the Model-View-Controller concept, which allows the programmer to change the user interface parts (View-Controller) independently of the underlying application specific objects. Of course, such change cannot be made at random in reality, as we have argued that the user interface is **not** something that can be considered independently of the other aspects of the application.

Chapter 6

User Interface Design: Advice to the Designer

> Do not automate the work that you are engaged in, only the materials. If you like to draw, do not automate the drawing; rather program your personal computer to give you a new set of paints. If you like to play music, do not build a "player piano"; instead program yourself a new kind of instrument. (Alan Kay)[1]

This chapter contains my conclusions. An obvious question to ask is: *What do the readers know about user interfaces and their design, now, that they would not have known without reading this book?* Was it worth the effort for the readers to have worked their way through it, and was it worth the effort for me to have written it? My goal has been to elaborate on the theory about design (of user interfaces) to make it contain ideas of hands-on experiences and prototyping that have so far only been empirically based. In short, the idea has been to look into the possibilities of bringing the theory up-to-date with the best of existing practical knowledge. At the same time, the prototypical or ideal cases described here, as well as the theoretical ideas, can probably help designers of computer applications change their design practice to do better user interface design.

The chapter is structured as follows: a summary of the conclusions, at a theoretical as well as a more practical level; a presentation and discussion of some recommendations to designers; and a discussion of the possibilities and perspective provided by the human activity approach. The conclusions are meant to summarize the theoretical aspects of the book: What are user interfaces? What is design? The recommendations are meant to outline actions that should be taken to do better design and make better user interfaces. The aims are to help designers change their practice in order to make better user interfaces, based on the practice of the future users. With this type of concluding chapter, I hope to inspire readers not only to reflect on the conclusions, but also to change their practice as researchers or designers.

Conclusions

Seen in retrospect, the main goal of this book has been to redefine the user interface concept and to make this definition operational in design. Through the theoretical approach, the focus has been on *how the computer application appears to its user in use, with particular emphasis on the operational aspects of this appearance*. The distinction between operational and intentional aspects of use, applied in this context, suggests that we ought to talk about human *operation* of a computer application rather than human–computer interaction. The user interface can be defined as the software and hardware *supporting the human operation of the computer application* in a specific type of use activity, constituting some of the material conditions for triggering specific operations in a specific use situation. This triggering is part of the nonarticulable aspects of practice that play a special role in user interface design: We cannot deal with them without dealing with the specific use activities in which the artifact is to be applied. The relation to practice makes it possible to deal with user interfaces not just for the individual user but for groups who share a practice.

The definition stresses the difference between the use situation, where the computer-based artifact is operated on while the user focuses on some other object or subject, and the design situation, where the computer-based artifact is one of the objects.[2]

Theoretically, as well as practically, there is still much work to be done in the human activity approach to arrive at a more detailed understanding of the role of artifacts in collective work and the consequences of this for the design of artifacts. There is definitely a trend in research indicating that we are heading in a direction where computer support for collective work becomes increasingly important, but so far the ideas presented have been without any real theoretical setting. I find it obvious that the human activity approach can play a role in this. The problem with the basis of Leontjew's work might turn out to be that he only sees communication as a coordination of physical work. To continue with the communicative aspects, we might need to look for a different theoretical basis or supplement.

Before going into concrete details of the conclusions, it is also important to stress that the human activity approach means a farewell to human–computer interaction as language–what a human being does in relation to a computer application is inherently instrumental–and to the notion of the ideal computer application as simulating human behavior–the human being is capable of handling the artifact as what it is, a thing. Furthermore, as design must deal with more than the articulable aspects of practice, it is not sufficient to see design as description. The human activity approach shares this type of conclusions with the approaches of Winograd and Flores, Dreyfus and Dreyfus, and Ehn.[3]

The human activity theory has some far-reaching consequences for the relationship between the use-directed activities of design and the more technical activities, the implementation of the artifact. In traditional systems design practice, the use-directed activities get structured in a way that more or less ensures the possibility of implementing the envisioned artifact. The human activity approach's focus on the practice of use does not provide this automatic relation, thus, the technical considerations are not supported directly.

With these more general conclusions, let's move on to some more specific ones. The main purpose is to give specific answers to what has been achieved by the human activity approach. For the sake of completeness, I add that some of these conclusions are common also to more of the approaches discussed previously.

The user interface

The relationship between the user interface and the specific type of use activity is demonstrated in the following conclusion: *The user interface cannot be seen independently of the goal or object, or of the other conditions of the use activity.*

There are two types of consequences of this, one concerns the use of general recommendations or guidelines for the user interface, and the other concerns the possibilities of assessing the user interface.

1. We can give certain general recommendations for the user interface, which are based on general cultural characteristics of the human use of computers. However, we have no warranty that such recommendations are applicable in a specific case. This means that we can try to apply general principles in a specific case, but that the evaluation of the user interface may result in giving up on some of those general principles.

2. In the evaluation or assessment, we must be aware that the user interface only reveals itself, fully, *in use.*

The following three statements define the user interface:

1. The user interface constitutes the conditions for operations, which are determined through the artifact. Furthermore, by the support or prevention of certain operations, the user interface constitutes conditions for possible actions.

2. The user interface consists of conditions for operations toward the artifact and for operations toward subjects or objects through the artifact.

3. The user interface consists of physical, handling, and subject/object-directed aspects. The physical aspects support the physical adaption of the user to the artifact; the handling aspects, the operations directed toward the artifact, and the subject/object-directed aspects the operations toward an object or a subject through the artifact.

In Chapter 4, we saw that although it is the purpose of the handling aspects to avoid breakdowns that bring the artifact into the awareness of its user, it is also important to anticipate such breakdowns and make it possible for the user to shift her focus back to the object or subject. This supports, and gives new reasons for, the following conclusion:

The user must be able to handle the breakdowns with regards to the artifact within the domain of use. Support in these situations is part of the handling aspects, but also a matter of education.

We have also seen a close connection between the competence of the users and the user interface; competence both in a narrow sense of operating the artifact and more broadly in relation to the practice of the user: *What is a good user interface at one level of competence can prevent efficient use at another, be it a higher or a lower level of competence.* It is well known that user interfaces designed for experts can be difficult for novices, but in Chapter 4 I gave examples of the opposite case as well, that user interfaces designed for novices can prevent efficient use by the experienced or expert user.

From the discussions about learning, it seems that user interfaces based on physical objects, where the user can actually see and touch the real, physical objects, seem easier to learn than user interfaces based on tangible graphic objects, such as the Macintosh interface. These are, in turn, easier than more abstract or language-based user interfaces, depending, of course, on the specific conditions.

No matter which type of user interface is chosen, in the application of an artifact, some of the user's actions and operations are always instrumental. The physical aspects as well as the handling aspects support instrumental actions and operations. Natural language interfaces aim to make instrumental aspects (i. e. handling aspects) communicative. In my perception, this is impossible or self-contradictory. If, however, the goal of the activity is achieved through communication, the communicative side is supported through the subject-directed aspects. The subject/object-directed aspects support communicative operations and actions when directed toward subjects; similarly, they support instrumental operations and actions when directed toward objects.

In Chapter 4, I demonstrated that it is possible to define the user interface technically in a way that is complementary to the use derived definition given here. Such terms as flexibility, consistency and simplicity can be defined in relation to the use activity. *Flexibility* has to do with the possibilities of shifting focus among objects and subjects, but also with the possibilities of achieving the same goal by different paths (different actions and operations). *Consistency* means that the computer responds to the actions of the user in the same way in situations that are the same to the user. *Simplicity,* refers to how many actions it takes for the user to achieve a certain goal.

From the comparison of the text editors Microsoft WORD and MacWrite, we know that simplicity in the handling aspects might contradict flexibility in the subject/object-directed aspects.

The design activity

As viewed by the human activity approach and in keeping with the ideas of, for example, Ehn or Winograd and Flores,[4] the design activity is characterized by a conflicting encounter among different practices, different needs for articulation of operations and their material conditions, and so forth. In this encounter, design becomes rooted in existing use practice, at the same time as it becomes possible to take steps to change the practice of use by means of the practice of the designers and groups of users.[5] *In design, we must handle different practices, at least that of the users and that of the designers.*

Only users, that is, human beings who share the practice of the group of future users, can evaluate all aspects of the user interface in design. This is quite a serious and challenging problem for design–to deal with a not yet existing practice. One place to start is to let the users and their practice be the origin for design. In design of the user interface, we must be able to handle all aspects of practice, the articulable as well as the nonarticulable, the instrumental as well as the communicative side.

User interface design is not something that should take place late in the design process after all the important decisions, but rather it is something that should be ongoing throughout the design process. From the point of view of use, user interface design is the main activity in design, together with the design of other physical and social surroundings. The technical description of the artifact must be derived from this. User interface design cannot be conducted independently of the rest of the design process, by so-called user interface experts, because this prevents the mutual learning process from taking place. This does not, however, exclude the need for competence in design, rather the work of the user interface experts must be integrated with the rest of the design process in cooperation with users.

Design means conceptualization of former operations and creation of new ones. Furthermore, design may mean automation of former human operations. Design deals with operations and the conditions by which they are triggered. We design new conditions for the collective as well as the individual activity. As design originates from the practice of use, *the design activity must be structured according to the use practice and not according to the technical components of the user interface*[6] or any other abstract or formal framework.

The human activity approach supports the idea that design is both construction of the future artifact and communication about it. The materialized visions constructed in the design activity are means of triggering conceptualization about present or future practice, especially operations. Design of user interfaces is a process in which breakdowns serve to detect problems of the future use. In the design activity we try to anticipate breakdowns all the time. The design activity makes use of breakdowns while also aiming to create a situation with no breakdowns in the final use. If successful, design leads from many to few breakdowns in anticipation and use of the future artifact.

We can distinguish among different types of triggers that help approach or simulate the encounter with the material world in various ways:

Scenarios can be used to draw attention to the present practice of the users and to the aspects of this that will be changed due to the introduction of a new artifact. Scenarios are meant to be evaluated by reading. They cannot necessarily draw attention to how aspects of practice will be changed.

Prototypes can be used to let the user try out actions and operations, in a real or simulated setting, and thus experience (aspects of) the encounter with the material world.

Design methods

Design methods can be either prescriptions of how a total design process is to take place or prescriptions that aim at a specific part of the design activity. Methods can be characterized according to how they aim to create artifacts to support instrumental actions and operations or communicative ones. Furthermore, one can distinguish between methods that aim at artifacts for collective activities or for individual activities only. According to the discussions of Chapter 5, how a method is formulated in relation to these distinctions has consequences for the physical, the handling, and the subject/object-directed aspects of the user interface. The method's emphasis tells us how much it is possible to focus on these aspects and how they are dealt with by the particular method.

Methods can aim at exploiting the inherent capabilities of computers differently: *Products of the design activity are more or less active or passive externalized artifacts.* We can make the following conclusions about the methods examined in Chapter 5: The established methods for design of computer applications in general, and for user interface design in particular, do not intend to originate from the practice of the users. They are based on a detached observation and description of the work activity to be changed by the new artifact, and they apply some formalism of description in this description. Description methods, such as those of Yourdon or even Card, Moran and Newell[7] are not sufficiently capable of dealing with the user interface because they do not allow communication about the nonarticulable aspects of practice, the encounter with the material world.

It is important to derive methods that take into account the need to distinguish between mediation of the interpersonal relationship and of relationships between human beings and things. Furthermore, we need to derive methods that allow for the inclusion of different aspects of practice in design: the articulable as well as the nonarticulable, the instrumental as well as the communicative sides. Last, but not least, the human activity approach emphasizes and gives support for the following conclusion: *Good design methods must prescribe that the means applied in a specific design activity must originate from the use activity in question.* We cannot produce one method that can be used in the design of user interfaces for all types of applications.

Recommendations to the designer

In the following, I present and discuss some recommendations to the designer. The recommendations are primarily meant to present the specific recommendations of the human activity approach, but again, for reasons of totality, I include two more general recommendations. First, I present and discuss the recommendations one by one: for the user interface, for the design activity, and for design methods.

The user interface

I first present two main statements about quality of user interfaces. These statements arise directly from the definition of the user interface and the role of the artifact in use:

A good user interface allows the user to conduct an activity through different actions and operations depending on the user's repertoire of operations and the actual material conditions.

With a good user interface, neither the physical aspects nor the handling aspects give rise to actions in ordinary use situations. All actions should be directed toward their appropriate objects and subjects rather than toward the artifact.

Looking more specifically at the physical and the handling aspects, we saw examples in Chapter 4 of how a different design of these aspects can be used to avoid actions toward the artifact, that is to prevent breakdowns:

Delay in response must follow the actions of the user and should not appear in the middle of an operation.

Prompts must be used with care. They are useful in guiding a user through unfamiliar actions but may create breakdowns when they appear in the middle of operations.

Although the physical and handling aspects should not call for actions from the user, it is also important that they support the user if a breakdown occurs. How this is done relates directly to the competence and education of the user, but it is important that *error situations be handled within the domain of use practice*. It is important that *the user be able to retract or undo* her operations, if this is important in the handling of the objects or subjects. Proper facilities can prevent breakdowns toward the artifact. Help mechanisms, error handling mechanisms, and so forth, which *actively* aim to predict or explain the actions and operations of the users, are based on a formalization of the conditions for the triggering of certain operations and may spoil existing operations by not acting according to the experiences of the user each time. Help mechanisms, error handling mechanisms, and the like, must be under the control of the user.

Turning to the subject/object-directed aspects, the main recommendation is: *For all the objects and subjects of use, the subject/object-directed aspects must support the development of operations.* The subject/object-directed aspects have different characteristics depending on whether they are support for actions and operations toward subjects, or toward objects; whether they support use of instrumental actions and operations toward objects or use of communicative actions and operations toward subjects.

Furthermore, the subject/object-directed aspects must support ease of shifting between subjects/objects where this is necessary in the future use activity. This means, for example, that modes should be used with care and that the handling aspects of the artifact should be consistent for different subjects/objects. This does not mean that it is always possible to handle the artifact in the same way always, but that the same type of situations should be handled the same way.

The design activity

The recommendations for the design activity have different characteristics than those for the user interface. Because they are recommendations for actions, there are dos and don'ts derived from the discussions in the previous chapters. What is important in design, according to the human activity approach, is the appearance of the computer-based artifact to its users in use, on the individual as well as the collective levels. The emphasis is on the operational aspects of the artifact, on what we call design of the user interface.

We cannot design the user interface after determining a set of actions to be conducted, a set of intentions (what is often called the functionality), although we have some intentions in mind when initiating the design activity. Rather, the physical, the handling, and the subject/object-directed aspects must all be dealt with equally in design. Out of this, by after-design reflection, we can determine the possible intentions. The physical, the handling, and the subject/object-directed aspects of the user interface are equally important and often interdependent: The handling aspects cannot be fully determined without the physical aspects, and the subject/object-directed aspects cannot be fully determined without the handling aspects. At the same time, however, the subject/object-directed aspects place specific requirements on the physical and handling aspects, and so on. One of the consequences of this is that both hardware and software have to be considered throughout the process. Many design methods prescribe software to be considered before hardware, whereas this book shows that software and hardware are equally important for the appearance of the artifact, the user interface.

The human activity approach gives support for the following recommendations about the handling of practice in design: To deal with a not yet existing practice, *the use practice must be the origin for design.* This in turn means *involving users actively in design.*

The encounter of the practices of the designers and of the users is important for design but requires a process of mutual learning. Through this the possibilities of transcending existing practice is achieved. The learning about other practices and the potential conflicts between the practices open up new possibilities for artifacts, cultural techniques, language, and so forth that are not brought about through one practice alone. This process, as well as dealing with different aspects of the future use practice, requires new methods. In the discussions of this book, possible candidates for such new methods have been discussed, but this area need to be worked on further.

The human activity approach gives some general recommendations for the design of user interfaces:

1. Create possibilities for the users to try out the user interface through use, not only through reflection.

2. Anticipate the subjects and objects of the future activity and be aware of the shifts between them in use.

3. Anticipate the levels of competence of the future use, as well as the domains of competence.

4. Focus on the difference between frequent and less frequent situations of use to deal with flexibility, consistency, and simplicity of the user interface.

In connection with this, it is important that a person can be an expert or a novice within many different domains. As pointed out in Chapter 4, it is possible to become an expert MacWrite user but not an expert document editor by using MacWrite. To create high-quality documents, however, it is not sufficient to be an expert MacWrite user. Designing the user interface means determining the levels of competence where the artifact can be used without special problems (breakdowns). *Education needs to be designed* to make it possible for the users to get to these levels.

From the preceding chapters we have seen that general guidelines and recommendations about the user interface can be applied to create realistic visions of the future artifact. However, the requirements of the specific use activity are still more important and may overrule the general recommendations. Creating realistic visions is important in design, but ideal visions can play a role that is just as important in enhancing the imagination of both users and computer experts.

Design methods

Which design methods to recommend for design of user interfaces from the human activity approach is still a research issue. In the next section, I discuss some of the research to be undertaken to achieve better design methods. Here, I give a brief summary of the state of recommendations.

The main conclusion is that professional designers need a toolbox of different kinds of methods, some of which are support for refining other methods to a specific design situation. For a later, purely technical implementation of the final artifact, this type of method must be supplemented with, for example, programming and technical description methods, an issue that has not been touched upon here.

The mock-up, the exploratory programming, and the fourth-generation tool methods can be included in a toolbox of design methods that the professional designer has access to.

Mock-ups and computer-based prototypes can be applied to simulate the encounter with the material world.

Better mock-up and computer-based prototyping artifacts can be achieved by focusing on a specific application domain and use practice(s). Therefore, the general toolbox must provide basic components that support different styles of interaction and a variety of hardware components, such as pointing devices, and so on. Various techniques that can help the designer use a computer to simulate a user interface can be useful, for example, by showing a sequence of screen images one after the other as pictures or even as a kind of movie. The showing of such sequences could even be influenced by the steps taken by the user in the interaction. The toolbox must make it possible for the designer to adjust these general components to the domain of application in an actual design situation. Also, it must be possible for the designer to use exploratory programming techniques to change the components of the toolbox. To support the designer's practice in developing such methods, a set of concrete examples can be given as education material.

There is a tendency that the more advanced the computer support for the design activity is, the more specific it is concerning the types of user interfaces that can be developed. Therefore, in the early stages of design, choose design methods that are as general as possible when it comes to which kind of user interface to end up with. Later on, more specific techniques and artifacts can be chosen.

Scenarios can be used to bring about an awareness of the present practice of the users, and through this an awareness of possible changes. The toolbox may benefit from being supplemented by different scenario methods.

The potential of the framework

The next step in taking advantage of the framework and the previous recommendations is to get to some more operational design methods and prove, in practice, that they are better than the methods that we know already. In Chapter 5 and earlier in this chapter, I have indicated areas where I think we must look for such new methods. I find it beyond my means at the present time to create and test concrete methods that will take us in these directions. The project to be discussed in the following hopefully contributes to this objective.

The future?

The ideas of the human activity approach are included in the following project, called APLEX.[8] The project started as part of an overall program that deals with computer support in cooperative work.[9] The main goal of the APLEX project is to develop a general, computer-based prototyping environment to be applied in design of single-user as well as multiuser situations. The APLEX is to be used in the early stages of design to facilitate design by doing.

We envision an APLEX by means of which prototypes can be built of plugable standard components and pieces of code written in a high-level language. The plugable components range from simulation of a slide projector, fourth-generation type components, support for simulating pieces of underlying programs, support for simulating the capabilities and style of different computers, and so on. All of these components can be changed and adjusted to the specific use situation. Furthermore, the use of video signals and the like will be considered as means of simulating parts of a computer application, and likewise there will be possibilities of letting a human being simulate part of the computer's part of the interaction.

Surrounding this APLEX also prototypes of total use situations can be set up, for example, plays in which the computer-based prototypes are applied. The APLEX as well as design methods surrounding its use has been developed in the project, and the development continue[10].

The technical design of the APLEX is a research challenge, and so is the study of which types of products that this type of design strategy will lead to. From a human activity point of view, it is important to deal with the physical, as well as the handling and subject/object-directed aspects. It becomes a research challenge to develop methods to explore all three aspects of the computer application and the relationships among them. Similar considerations holds for the relationships between the collective and the individual activity.

It is also necessary to work theoretically and practically with prototyping in a multiuser setting and with requirements posed by different types of application domains. According to the human activity approach, the APLEX can support certain general recommendations but not enforce them. A consistent framework for the application of such is another research issue.

One of the initial steps in this research and design process was to explore difficulties and benefits of designing with users utilizing existing computer-based tools. In the experiments done thus far, we have used HyperCard. We apply a technique called *cooperative prototyping* to establish a design process where users participate actively and creatively. Among other experiments, we have designed a patient case record system for municipal dental clinics.[11] This patient record system combines administrative information with treatment-oriented information, utilizing direct representation of teeth on the screen. The users are mainly dental assistants working in dental clinics of public schools, with no previous computer experience. The experiments showed that it was possible to make a number of *direct manipulation* changes of prototypes in cooperation with the users, in interplay with their fluent worklike evaluation. However, breakdowns occurred in the prototyping process when we reached the limits of the direct manipulation support for modification. Despite these breakdowns, we conclude that a prototype used this way becomes a valuable vehicle for communication and engagement. The experiences from the experiment together with the last version of the prototype will be valuable input for a process aimed at implementing a good tool for the dental assistants.

It is not really the goal of the APLEX to help the programmer create the inside structure of the final programs, and it is a point that the functionality need not be fully evolved to give an impression of how the computer application will appear to its user. There may still be much work for programmers to turn a prototype into a real computer application. We have no experiences in how such a prototype works as a requirement specification, and perhaps we need to look for new methods for programmers to use to get from the prototype to a running computer application.

From ideal to reality?

Earlier we saw that the human activity approach plays a role in suggesting how design is to take place, both in refining concepts of user interface design and as an ideal or a prototypical case. The approach is normative because it states that if we want to design computer-based artifacts, there are some conditions under which design needs to take place. I have discussed the ideal setting for design as being consensus groups, but real-life design rarely takes place in this kind of setting. It is obvious that the human activity approach can be used, and misused, depending on the political conditions surrounding the design. I take the relativist position, in Hirschheim's[12] meaning of the word: I am optimistic about the possibilities of making better computer applications, but at the same time skeptical as to how they may be used. At least some negotiations and resources are required to set up the required type of design situations, but often the situation is much more complicated and requires the handling of different interests, and so forth. How this can be done–for example how technology agreements can be set up to regulate evolutionary or prototypical design, how the size, timewise and resourcewise, can be estimated for this type of projects–and similar problems need to be dealt with if we want to see better design taking place in real-life situations in the future. In general, this is not a matter of individual idealism but of collective bargaining and changing societal conditions.[13]

Despite this, I hope that I have come up with reasons and ideas for changing practice in order to make better user interfaces, with some ideas to how better design can take place, even in industry. Hopefully, designers will be able to make use of my recommendations to reconsider their practice regardless of the political conditions, because they want to do better design. Even more, I hope that the APLEX will contribute to this and that we will be able also to include aspects of the political conditions in the more long-term components of the project, because this new type of design will, in the end, require new types of strategies for the involved parties, unions and management.

Design is where the action is in the user interface

I chose the quote "Design is where the action is in the user interface" by Allen Newell as the opening line of this book. This was done to stress the fact that user interface design is an important area, one where much research needs to be done, and to acknowledge the opening up of cognitive science toward design.

However, this book has questioned whether the path of traditional cognitive science is the right one, and even so there seems to be more important problems concerning most of the traditional design approaches. If we stay with Newell, his concern is for how cognitive scientists/user interface experts exert the proper influence on the computer application, and he concludes that when the functionality has been designed, the computer scientists/experts must take over and act on design. With the human activity approach, this type of consideration is turned upside down: It is not a matter of designing the user interface after the functionality, but of getting to a design approach where it is almost possible to design how the artifact will appear to the users in use, including also the social and physical surroundings of the artifact use. Design of any other aspect or issue, such as technical features, must be derived from this. The human activity approach has resulted in an understanding of computer applications where the user interface plays a much more fundamental role. A formulation of the last line could be the following:

The user interface is where the action is in design.

---

1 Kay, A. (1977). Microelectronics and the personal computer. *Scientific American, 237,* 230–244.

2 There are situations in use where the computer based artifact becomes the object of use, these are exactly the situations where the user interface fails. Furthermore, there are some design situations where the artifact to be designed is applied at the same time, for example, the use of a programming environment to design the same programming environment.

3 Winograd, T., & Flores C. F. (1986). *Understanding computers and cognition: A new foundation for design.* Norwood, NJ: Ablex, Dreyfus, H., & Dreyfus, S. (1986). *Mind over machine: The power of human intuition and expertise in the era of the computer.* Glasgow: Basil Blackwell, Ehn, P. (1988). *Work-oriented design of computer artifacts.* Falköping, Sweden: Arbetslivscentrum/Almqvist & Wiksell International.

4 Ehn or Winograd & Flores, ibid.

5 If the users are also the designers, this is both good and potentially bad; good because it is easy to start from the practice of the users, potentially bad because there are no outsiders to uncover the blindness created by the common background of the designers/users.

6 This goes not only for the design activity. The user interface needs to be structured according to the use activity as well.

7 Yourdon, E. (1982). *Managing the systems life cycle.* London: Yourdon, or Card, S., Moran, T., & Newell, A. (1983). *The psychology of human–computer interaction.* Hillsdale, NJ: Lawrence Erlbaum Associates, despite their initial talk about trying out prototypes.

[8] See Bødker, S., Ehn, P., Lindskov Knudsen, J., Kyng, M., Halskov Madsen, K. (1988). Computer Support for Cooperative Design. In D. Tatar (Ed.). *CSCW 88. Proceedings from the Second CSCW* (pp. 377-394) or Bøgh Andersen, P., Bødker, S., Ehn, P., Holmquist, B., Kyng, M., Halskov Madsen, K., Lindskov Knudsen, J., & Sørgaard, P. (1987). *Research Programme on Computer Support in Cooperative Design and Communication*, University of Aarhus. Unpublished manuscript.

[9] The program is a long term multidisciplinary research effort conducted jointly by the Department of Computer Science and the Institute of Information and Media Science, University of Aarhus.

[10]Greenbaum, J. & Kyng, M. (Eds.)(in press). *Design at Work: Approaches to Collaborative Design*. Hillsdale, NJ: Lawrence Erlbaum Associates.

[11] Bødker, S., & Grønbæk, K. (1989). Cooperative prototyping experiments: Users and designers envision a dentist case record system. In J. Bowers & S. Benford (Eds.), *Proceedings of the First European Conference on Computer-Supported Cooperative Work, EC-CSCW* (pp. 343–357).

[12] Hirschheim, R. A. (1986). The effect of a priori views on the social implications of computing: The case of office automation. *Computing Surveys, 18(2)*, 165–195.

[13] This is a place where I think Hirschheim, ibid. is wrong in his view of the Scandinavian trade union approach (the collective resource approach, see Ehn, P., & Kyng, M. (1987). The collective resource approach to systems design. In G. Bjerknes, P. Ehn, & M. Kyng (Eds.). *Computers and democracy: A Scandinavian challenge.* (pp. 17–58), Aldershot, UK: Avebury. He is right when he calls the tradition a relativist position in the presented meaning of the word, but when he characterizes this position as dealing with freedom, affection, recognition, etc., of the individual, he forgets the fundamental distinction, which I discussed in Chapter 1, between idealism and materialism.

Acknowledgments

It is not possible for me to list and thank each individual who helped me with this book: students and colleagues at DAIMI, colleagues from the Swedish Center for Working Life and the Royal Institute of Technology, Stockholm, who participated in the UTOPIA and DIALOG projects, members of the SCG/SCL at Xerox PARC; the people at Aarhus Polytechnics, colleagues from the Institute of Psychology and from the Institute of Information and Media Science in Aarhus.

I appreciate the help from long-time friends who work as computer scientists in industry or as consultants; and I gratefully acknowledge the encouraging support from a group of women computer scientists who insisted on the importance of getting more women to do computer science teaching and research.

Karen Møller helped me type and edit the manuscript. Morten Kyng was my supervisor, and he, Brian Mayoh, and Ole Lehrmann Madsen constituted my *licentiat* committee. Jan Holdam did a tremendous job commenting on the final draft of the original dissertation, as did Preben Mogensen on this book.

John Kammersgaard and I worked together on the Aarhus Polytechnics case and developed many of the early ideas from which this book has evolved. Most of the practical ideas about user interface design in the UTOPIA project was developed by the project group in Stockholm. I am very grateful for the possibility of sharing their reflections. I also want to thank Horst Oberquelle for many encouraging discussions, and Randy Trigg for many valuable and constructive comments.

I owe special thanks to Morten Kyng and Pelle Ehn for creating an interesting environment for many exciting discussions, as well as for many hours of detailed comments and good advice.

Bibliography

Andersen, C., Krogh-Jespersen, F., & Petersen, A. (1972). *SYSKON–en bog om konstruktion af datamatiske systemer (Vols. 1-2)* [SYSKON–A book about construction of computer systems]. Odense: G. E. C. Gads Forlag.

Andersen, N. E., Kensing, F., Lassen, M., Lundin, J., Mathiassen, L., Munk-Madsen, A., & Sørgaard, P. (1990). *Professional system development: Experience, ideas, and action.* Englewood Cliffs, NJ: Prentice Hall.

Bannon, L. (1986). Computer-mediated communication. In D. A. Norman & S. W. Draper (Eds.), *User–centered system design* (pp. 433–452). Hillsdale, NJ: Lawrence Erlbaum Associates.

Bannon, L., & Bødker, S. (in press). Beyond the interface: Encountering artifacts in use. In J. Carroll. (Ed.), *Designing interaction: Psychological theory at the human–computer interface* (publication expected 1990).

Bartholdy, M., Nordquist, C., & Romberger, S. (1987). *Studie av DATORSTÖDD BILD-BEHANDLING på Aftonbladet* [A study of computer-supported image processing at Aftonbladet] (UTOPIA Report No. 21). Stockholm: Arbetslivscentrum.

Bisgaard, O., Mogensen, P., Nørby, M., & Thomsen, M. (1989). *Systemudvikling som lærevirksomhed, konflikter som basis for organisationel udvikling* [Systems development as learning activity, conflicts as the origin of organizational development] (DAIMI IR-88). Århus: University of Aarhus.

Bjerknes, G., Ehn, P., & Kyng, M. (Eds.) (1987). *Computers and democracy: A Scandinavian challenge.* Aldershot, UK: Avebury.

Borman, L., & Curtis, B. (Eds.) (1985). Human factors in computing systems. *Proceedings*, ACM.

Bødker, S. (1989). A human activity approach to user interfaces. *Human–Computer Interaction, 4(3)*, 171–195.

Bødker, S., Ehn, P., Kammersgaard, J., Kyng, M., & Sundblad, Y. (1987). A Utopian experience. In G. Bjerknes et al., 1987 (pp. 251–278).

Bødker, S., Ehn, P., Lindskov Knudsen, J., Kyng, M., Halskov Madsen, K. (1988). Computer Support for Cooperative Design. In D. Tatar (Ed.). *CSCW 88. Proceedings from the Second CSCW* (pp. 377-394)

Bødker, S., Ehn, P., Romberger, S., & Sjögren, D. (Eds.) (1985). *Graffiti 7. The UTOPIA project: An alternative in text and images.* Stockholm:Arbetslivcentrum.

Bødker, S., & Grønbæk, K. (1989). Cooperative prototyping experiments: Users and designers envision a dentist case record system. In J. Bowers & S. Benford (Eds.), *Proceedings of the First European Conference on Computer-Supported Cooperative Work, EC-CSCW* (pp. 343–357).

Bødker, S., & Hammerskov, J. (1982). *Grafisk systembeskrivelse* [Graphical systems description] (DAIMI IR-33, IR-34, and IR-35). Århus: University of Aarhus.

Bødker, S., & Kammersgaard, J. (1984). *Interaktionsbegreber* [Interaction concepts]. Unpublished manuscript.

Bøgh Andersen, P. (1984). *Edb-teknologi set i medieperspektiv* [Computer technology seen in a media perspective]. The Joint Studies of Humanities and Computer Science, University of Aarhus. Unpublished manuscript.

Bøgh Andersen, P., Bødker, S., Ehn, P., Holmquist, B., Kyng, M., Halskov Madsen, K., Lindskov Knudsen, J., & Sørgaard, P. (1987). *Research Programme on Computer Support in Cooperative Design and Communication*, University of Aarhus. Unpublished manuscript.

Card, S. K., English, W. K., & Burr, B. J. (1978). Evaluation of a mouse, rate controlled isometric joystick, step keys, and text keys for text selection on a CRT. *Ergonomics 21(8)*, 601–614.

Card, S., Moran, T., & Newell, A. (1980). The keystroke-level model for user performance time with interactive systems. *Communications of the ACM, 23(7)*, 396–410.

Card, S., Moran, T., & Newell, A. (1983). *The psychology of human–computer interaction.* Hillsdale, NJ: Lawrence Erlbaum Associates.

Carroll, J. (Ed.) (1987). *Interfacing thought, cognitive aspects of human–computer interaction.* Cambridge, MA: MIT Press.

Carroll, J. (1989a). *Evaluation, description, and invention: Paradigms for human–computer interaction* (RC 13926 [#62583]). Yorktown Heights, N.Y.: IBM.

Carroll, J. (1989b). Taking artifacts seriously. In S. Maass & H. Oberquelle (Eds.), *Software ergonomie '89* (pp. 36–50). Stuttgart: Tentner.

Carroll, J. & Campbell, R. (1989). *Artifacts as Psychological Theories: the case of human-computer interaction.* (IBM RC 13454 (# 60225)), Yorktown Heights: IBM.

Caspersen, J., Gaardbo, P., Kjær, J., Klötzl, J., Krogh, P.E., & Mathiasen, L. (1985). *Description techniques for interactive systems.* Ålborg Universitetscenter. Unpublished manuscript.

Christiansen, E. (1989). *Den realistiske vision* [The realistic vision]. Unpublished doctoral dissertation, Ålborg Universitetscenter, Denmark.

Churchman, C. W. (1968). *The systems approach.* New York: Dell.

Cole, M., & Maltzman, I. (Eds.) (1969). *A handbook of contemporary Soviet psychology.* New York: Basic.

DeMarco, T. (1979). *Structured analysis and system specification.* London: Yourdon.

Dreyfus, H., & Dreyfus, S. (1986). *Mind over machine: The power of human intuition and expertise in the era of the computer.* Glasgow: Basil Blackwell.

Dzida, W. (no date). *The IFIP model for user interfaces* (GMD-F2G2). Bonn: GMD.

Ehn, P. (1988). *Work-oriented design of computer artifacts.* Falköping, Sweden: Arbetslivscentrum/Almqvist & Wiksell International (2nd edition: Lawrence Erlbaum Associates).

Ehn, P., Eriksson, B., Eriksson, M., Frenckner, K., & Sundblad, Y. (1984). *Utformning av datorstödd ombrytning för dagstidningar* [Computer-aided page makeup for newspapers] (UTOPIA Report no. 12). Stockholm: Arbetslivscentrum.

Ehn, P., & Kyng, M. (1984). A tool perspective on design of interactive computer support for skilled workers. In M. Sääksjärvi (Ed.), *Proceedings from the Seventh Scandinavian Research Seminar on Systemeering* (pp. 211–242). Helsinki: Helsinki Business School.

Ehn, P., & Kyng, M. (1987). The collective resource approach to systems design. In G. Bjerknes et al., 1987 (pp. 17–58).

Ehn, P., Kyng, M., & Sundblad, Y. (1981). *Training, technology, and product from the quality of work perspective, A Scandinavian research project on union based development of and training in computer technology and work organization, especially text and image processing in the graphic industry* (UTOPIA Report No. 2). Stockholm: Arbetslivscentrum.

Ehn, P., & Sandberg, Å. (1979). God utredning [Good investigation]. In Å. Sandberg (Ed.), *Utredning och förändring i förvaltningen,* (pp. 13-57). Stockholm: Liber.

Engeström, Y. (1987). *Learning by expanding.* Helsinki: Orienta-Konsultit.

Fischer, G., Lembke, A., & Schwab, T. (1984). Active help systems. In T. Green, M. Tauber, & G. van der Veer, (Eds.), *Cognitive ergonomics, mind and computer.* Proceedings of the Second European Conference on Cognitive Ergonomics, Mind, and Computer (pp. 116–131). Berlin: Springer Verlag.

Fischer, G., Lembke, A., & Schwab, T. (1985). Knowledge-based help systems. In L. Borman & B. Curtis, 1985 (pp. 161-167).

Floyd, C. (1984). A systematic look at prototyping. In R. Budde, K. Kühlenkamp, L. Mathiassen, & H. Züllighoven (Eds.), *Approaches to prototyping* (pp. 1-18). Berlin: Springer Verlag.

Foley, J. D., & van Dam, A. (1982). *Fundamentals of interactive computer graphics.* Reading, MA: Addison-Wesley.

Fox Keller, E. (1985). *Reflections on gender and science.* New Haven, CT: Yale University Press.

Gal'perin, P. Y. (1969). Stages in the development of mental acts. In M. Cole & I. Maltzman, 1969 (pp. 249-273).

Goldberg, A. (1984). *SMALLTALK-80: The interactive programming environment.* Reading, MA: Addison-Wesley.

Goldberg, A., & Robson, D. (1983). *Smalltalk-80: The language and its implementation*. Reading, MA: Addison-Wesley.

Greenbaum, J. (1987). *The head and the heart*. (DAIMI PB-237). Århus: University of Aarhus.

Greenbaum, J. & Kyng, M. (Eds.)(in press). *Design at Work: Approaches to Collaborative Design*. Hillsdale, NJ: Lawrence Erlbaum Associates, in press.

Göranzon, B. (Ed.) (1984). *Datautvecklingens filosofi* [The philosophy of computer development]. Malmö, Sweden: Carlsson & Jönsson.

Göranzon, B., Gullers, P., Mäkilä, K., Svensson, P., & Thollander, L. (1983). *Datorn som verktyg–krav och ansvar vid systemutveckling* [The computer as a tool]. Lund: Studentlitteratur.

Hammond, N., Helms Jørgensen, A., Maclean, A., Barnard, P., & Long, J. (1983). Design practice and interface usability: Evidence from interviews with designers. In A. Janda, 1983 (pp. 40–44).

Hirschheim, R. A. (1986). The effect of a priori views on the social implications of computing: The case of office automation. *Computing Surveys, 18(2)*, 165–195.

Holbæk-Hanssen, E., Håndlykken, P., & Nygaard, K. (1975). *System description and the DELTA language*. Oslo: Norwegian Computing Center.

Hydén, L.-C. (1981). *Psykologi och materialism. Introduktion till den materialistiska psykologin* [Psychology and materialism. An Introduction to materialistic psychology]. Stockholm: Prisma.

Janda, A. (Ed.) (1983). Human factors in computing systems. *Proceedings*, ACM.

Juul-Jensen, U. (1973) *Videnskabsteori* (Vol. 2) [The philosophy of science]. Copenhagen: Berlinske Forlag.

Kammersgaard, J. (1985a). *Four different perspectives on human–computer interaction* (DAIMI PB-203). Århus: University of Aarhus.

Kammersgaard, J. (1985b). On models and their role in the use of computers. *Preceedings of the Aarhus Conference on Development and Use of Computer-based Systems and Tools* (pp. 241–250). Århus: University of Aarhus.

Karpatschof, B. (1984). Grænsen for automatisering [The Limit of automation]. *Psyke og Logos, 2,* 201–220.

Kay, A. (1977). Microelectronics and the personal computer. *Scientific American, 237,* 230–244.

Kay, A., & Goldberg, A. (1981). A personal dynamic media. In A. I. Wasserman (Ed.), *Software development environment* (pp. 82–92). New York: IEEE.

Knuth, D. E. (1979). *TEX and METAFONT: New directions in typesetting.* Bedford, MA: Digital Press.

Krasner, G. (Ed.) (1983). *SMALLTALK-80: Bits of history, words of advice.* Reading, MA: Addison-Wesley.

Kristensen, B. H., Bollesen, N., & Sørensen, O. L. (1986). *Retningslinier for valg af faglige strategier på kontorområdet–et case studie over Århus tekniske Skoles kontorautomatiseringsprojekt* [Guidelines for trade union strategies in the office area: A case study of the office automation project of the Aarhus School of Polytechnics]. Unpublished master's thesis, Department of Computer Science, University of Aarhus.

Leontjew, A. N. (1978). *Activity, consciousness, and personality.* Englewood Cliffs, NJ: Prentice-Hall.

Leontjew, A. N. (1981a). The problem of activity in psychology. In J. V. Wertsch, 1981 (pp. 57-70).

Leontjew, A. N. (1981b). *Problems of the development of the mind.* Moscow: Progress.

Lundeberg, M, Goldkuhl, G., & Nilsson, A. (1978). *Systemering* [Systemeering]. Lund: Studentlitteratur.

Lundequist, J. (1982). *Norm och modell* [Norm and model]. Unpublished doctoral dissertation, The Royal Institute of Technology, Stockholm.

Mathiassen, L. (1981). *Systemudvikling og systemudviklingsmetode* [Systems development and systems development method] (DAIMI PB-136). Århus: University of Aarhus.

Miller, R. (1968). Response time in man–computer conversational transactions. *Fall Joint Computer Conference* (pp. 267–277).

Moran, T. P. (1981). The command language grammar. A representation for the user interface of interactive computer systems. *International Journal of Man–Machine Studies, 15(1)*, 3–50.

Mumford, E. (1987). Sociotechnical systems design: Evolving theory and practice. In G. Bjerknes et al., 1987 (pp. 59–76).

Newell, A. & Card, S. (1985). The prospects for psychological science in human–computer interaction, *Human Computer Interaction, 1*, 209–242.

Newman, W. M., & Sproull, R. F. (1979). *Principles of interactive computer graphics* (2nd ed.). Tokyo: McGraw-Hill.

Norman, D. (1988). *The psychology of everyday things*. New York: Basic.

Norman, D. A., & Draper, S. W. (Eds.) (1986). *User–centered system design*. Hillsdale, NJ: Lawrence Erlbaum Associates.

Oberquelle, H. (1985). *Semi-formal graphic modelling of dialog systems* (Bericht Nr. FBI-HH-B-113/85). Hamburg: Universität Hamburg, FB Informatik.

Oberquelle, H., Kupka, I., & Maass, S. (1983). A view of human–machine communication and cooperation. *International Journal of Man–Machine Studies, 19(4)*, 309–333.

Parnas, D. L. (1969). On the use of transition diagram in the design of a user interface for an interactive computer system. *Proceedings. ACM 24th National Conference* (pp. 378–385).

Polanyi, M. (1967). *Personal knowledge*. London: Routledge & Kegan Paul.

Reisner, P. (1981). Formal grammar and human factors design of an interactive graphics system. *IEEE Transactions on Software Engineering, SE-7*, 229–240.

Roberts, T. L., & Moran, T. P. (1983). The evaluation of text editors: Methodology and empirical results. *Communications of the ACM 26(4)*, 265–283.

Shiel, B. (1983). Power tools for programmers. *Datamation, 29(2)*, 131-144.

Shneiderman, B. (1979). Human factors experiments in designing interactive systems. *Computer, December*, 9–19.

Shneiderman, B. (1982). Multiparty grammars and related features for defining interactive systems. *IEEE Transactions on Systems, Man, and Cybernetics, SMC-12*, 148–154.

Shneiderman, B. (1983). Direct manipulation: A step beyond programming languages. *Computer, August,* 57–69.

SIS handbok 113. (1973). *Riktslinjer för administrativ systemutveckling* [Guidelines for administrative systems development]. Stockholm: SIS.

Stefik, M., Bobrow, D. G., Lanning, S., & Tatar, D. (1986). WYSIWIS revisited: Early experiences with multi-user interfaces. *Proceedings from CSCW '86* (pp. 276–290). Conference on Computer-Supported Cooperative Work, December 3–5, 1986, Austin, Texas.

Suchman, L. (1987). *Plans and situated actions: The problem of human–machine communication.* Cambridge: Cambridge University Press.

Suchman, L., & Wynn, E. (1984). Procedures and problems in the office. *Office: Technology and People, 2,* 133–154.

Sundblad, Y. (Ed.) (1987). *Quality and interaction in computer-aided graphic design* (UTOPIA Report No. 15). Stockholm: Arbetslivscentrum.

Tanner, P., & Buxton, W. (1985). Some issues in future User Interface Management System (UIMS) development. In G. Pfaff (Ed.), *User Interface Management Systems* (pp. 67–80). Berlin: Springer Verlag.

Thesen, A., & Beringer, D. (1986). Goodness-of-fit in the user–computer interface: A hierarchical control framework related to "friendliness." *IEEE Transactions on Systems, Man, and Cybernetics, SMC-16(7),* 158-162.

Thomas, J. C., Jr. (1978). A design-interpretation analysis of natural English with applications to man–computer interaction. *International Journal of Man–Machine Studies 10(6),* 151–167.

Tikhomirov, O. K. (1981). The psychological consequences of computation. In J. V. Wertsch, 1981 (pp. 256-278).

Trigg, R., Moran, T. P., & Halasz, F. G. (1987). Adaptability and tailorability in NoteCards. In H. C. Bullinger & B. Shackel (Eds.), *Human–computer interaction: INTERACT '87* (pp. 723–728). Amsterdam: Elsevier/North-Holland.

Wasserman, A. I. (1979). USE: A methodology for the design and development of interactive information systems. In H.-J. Schneider (Ed.), *Formal models and practical tools for information system design*, (pp. 31–50). Amsterdam: North-Holland.

Wasserman, A. I. (1980). Software tools and the user software engineering project. In W. E. Riddle & R. E. Fairley (Eds.), *Software development tools* (pp. 93–113). Berlin: Springer Verlag.

Wertsch, J. V. (Ed.) (1981). *The concept of activity in Soviet psychology.* Armonk, NY: Sharpe.

Whiteside, J., & Wixon, D. (1987). Discussion: Improving human–computer interaction–A quest for cognitive science. In J. Carroll, 1987 (pp. 353-365).

Winograd, T., & Flores C. F. (1986). *Understanding computers and cognition: A new foundation for design.* Norwood, NJ: Ablex.

Wittgenstein, L. (1953). *Philosophical investigations.* Oxford: Oxford University Press.

Yourdon, E. (1982). *Managing the systems life cycle.* London: Yourdon.

Index

Author index

Appendix

A brief description of MacWrite and Microsoft WORD

The purpose of this appendix is not to give a thorough description of the two computer applications and their use, but rather to point at what are important characteristics of the two applications for the analysis of their user interfaces. The intention is not that the reader will be able to learn to use the two text editors from this description; better material exists for this. The main idea of this description is to provide the reader with an understanding of *how* the application is used. This can, of course, only be fully experienced through the reader's own use.

MacWrite[1] and Microsoft WORD[2] share many characteristics because they are both designed to live up to the standard Macintosh user interface (Fig. A1 and Fig. A2).[3] They have a menu of pull-down menus at the top, a scrollbar with which to move vertically in the document on the right (in WORD one can scroll horizontally via the bar at the bottom of the screen), and a relatively big window where the document is displayed in the middle of the screen, which takes most of the space. The pull-down menus work as follows: by selecting an item in the main menu, a new menu, with different entries, opens for selection.

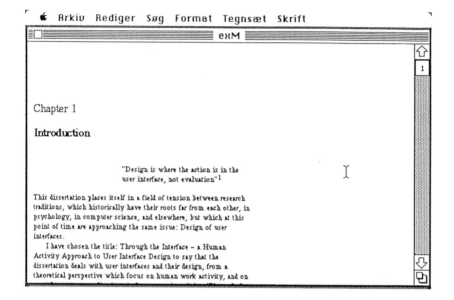

Fig. A1. MacWrite with text window open, the menu to pull down at the top, scrollbar to the right

The text editors both use the Macintosh input devices: the keyboard and the mouse with one button. In both cases, text can be entered by placing the cursor with the mouse, and typing (Figs. A3 and A4). Cutting, pasting, and copying of text can be done by selecting text with the mouse and issuing a command from the edit menu (Figs. A5 and A6).[4] Graphics can be pasted into the document and scaled/positioned, but the contents cannot be edited. The specific characteristics of the text editors are described in the following sections.

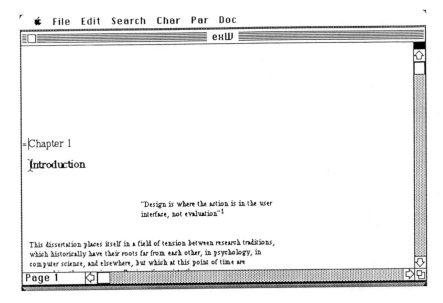

Fig. A2. Microsoft WORD with text window open, the menu to pull down at the top, scrollbar to the right and bottom

Through its wide register of ways of issuing the same commands, WORD allows the users to evolve different patterns of operations and, in many cases, use shortcuts for the routine cases. MacWrite is not as flexible, neither in this case, nor when it comes to exploiting the text editors to create good typographical quality.[5] Particularly when it comes to line spacing and to the choice of font sizes, more flexibility is needed.

For both WORD and MacWrite it is relatively easy to become expert in their use. WORD, however, has more to offer a skilled secretary, professional word processor, or typographer who is, or wants to be, an expert document designer. Furthermore, MacWrite is obviously designed to support less skilled document designers and is an example demonstrating that when such designers want to develop their competence, what-you-see-is-what-you-get soon becomes what-you-see-is-all-you-got.

⌘ Arkiv Rediger Søg Format Tegnsæt Skrift

exM

use of computer applications in human work activity. Through the Interface' tell us that a computer application, from the user's perspective, is not something that the user operates on but something that the user operates through on other objects or subjects. In this dissertation, the user interface is seen as the parts of software and hardware which support this effect. When I use a text editor to write this chapter, the user interface supports my work on the form and content of the document, and if it is a good user interface I am capable of forgetting that I actually work with a computer between the document and myself.

The traditions

I base this dissertation on one of the traditions, the tradition which has often been called the Aarhus-Oslo school. Its field has been systems development in its widest meaning: analysis and design of computer based systems and their surrounding organizations as well as the study of impacts of such systems on labor[2]. The background of this school has been a critical attitude towards traditional phase-oriented systems development methods[3], which have in turn mainly been dealing with development of large batch-oriented computer systems[4] from a management perspective.

The character of computer applications are, however, changing from large mainframe computers to personal workstations, from data-entry and number-crunching to interactive, graphics oriented

Fig. A3. The text with which one works: the | indicates the point where insertion of text is going to happen.

⌘ Arkiv Rediger Søg Format Tegnsæt Skrift

exM

use of computer applications in human work activity. Through the Interface' tell us that a computer application, from the user's perspective, is not something that the user operates on but something that the user operates through on other objects or subjects. In this dissertation, the user interface is seen as the parts of software and hardware which support this effect. When I use a text editor to write this chapter, the user interface supports my work on the form and content of the document, and if it is a good user interface I am capable of forgetting that I actually work with a computer between the document and myself.

The good old traditions

I base this dissertation on one of the traditions, the tradition which has often been called the Aarhus-Oslo school. Its field has been systems development in its widest meaning: analysis and design of computer based systems and their surrounding organizations as well as the study of impacts of such systems on labor[2]. The background of this school has been a critical attitude towards traditional phase-oriented systems development methods[3], which have in turn mainly been dealing with development of large batch-oriented computer systems[4] from a management perspective.

The character of computer applications are, however, changing from large mainframe computers to personal workstations, from data-entry and number-crunching to interactive, graphics oriented

Fig. A4. Text after typing some words ('good old')

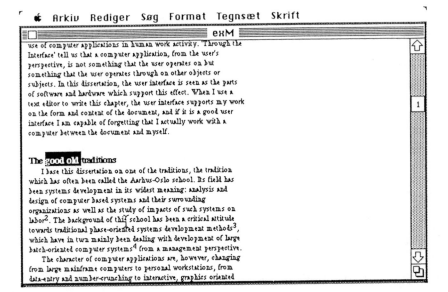

Fig. A5. Selection of text by painting with the mouse, the selected text is shown in inverse

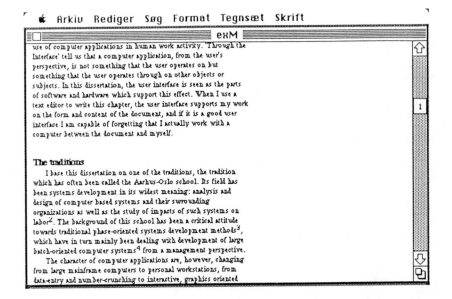

*Fig. A6. Text after deleting the words 'good old,' using the command "cut" from the **Rediger** (Edit) menu. Hitting the backspace key has the same effect*

MacWrite

The format of the document (margin width, etc.) can be changed by means of
a ruler, which has some icons attached to it (Fig. A7). The format created this
way is in effect until the next ruler appears or is placed. By pulling the
margin marks of the ruler with the mouse, we can change the margins as we
do on a typewriter (Fig. A8). Tabs can be set the same way. Line width and
justification can be changed by clicking the mouse button with the cursor
pointing at the icon. The icons are quite self-explanatory (Fig. A9). Line
width and justification can also be changed by entering one of the pull-down
menus or by key-stroke commands.

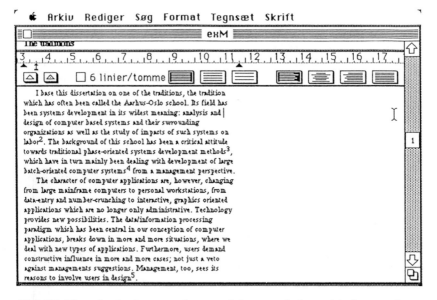

*Fig. A7. The ruler is shown at the top of the text window with the margin
marks shown together with icons indicating line width and justification*

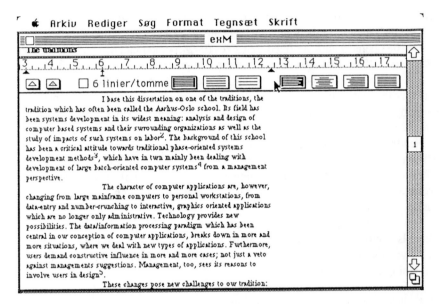

Fig. A8. Format changed by pulling the margin marks. The left indentation of the first line of a paragraph is now very big

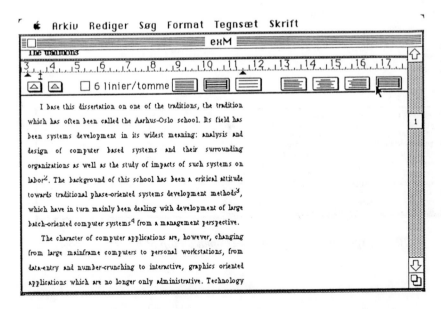

Fig. A9. Change of line width and justification from single line spacing and left justification to one and a half line spacing and full justification

Fonts, font size, and style are changed by selection in the *tegnsæt* ('character') menu; for the font style there are also key-stroke commands. MacWrite operates with six fixed font sizes (9–24 points) independent of which sizes of the font are available on the computer (i. e. we can only choose Boston in 9–24 points even though the real font size is 36 points). Whether the font is available in the selected size or scaled is indicated in the menu by the use of different font styles. The font style menu items are icons that show the text with the specific style.

Headings and footings are created through a special window (Fig. A10), where the text is typed and where page number and time stamp can be placed. After the window is closed, the heading will appear as part of the text in the document (Fig. A11), although it can be changed only through the special window.

In the scrollbar of the document it is indicated on which page we work. There is a maximum document length of 8.5 pages, according to the manual. In the version used here, the maximum length of the document appears to be something like 20 pages.

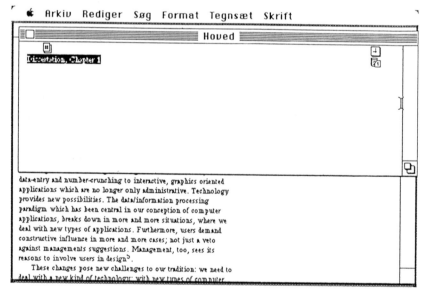

Fig. A10. The special heading window is open on top of the text window

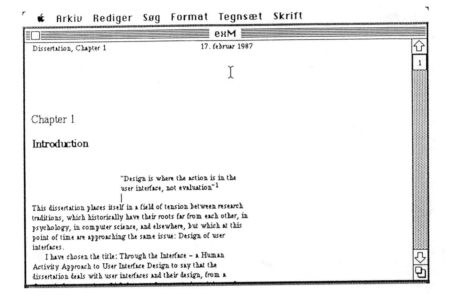

Fig. A11. The main window after creating a heading, and closing the heading window

Microsoft WORD

The formats of the document–through WORD–can be changed in the following ways: The margin sizes can be adjusted both for the document in general (Fig. A12) and for individual paragraphs.[6] For individual paragraphs, a form sheet is used (Fig. A13). On this form sheet, one can also specify the line spacing, not just in single/double spacing but in points as well as in other units. Extra space before and after paragraphs can be specified as well (Figs. A14 and A15).

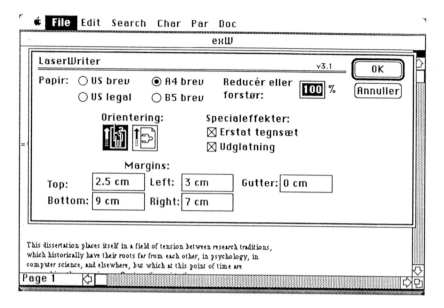

Fig. A12. Setting up format for the document in general, applying "page set-up" in the "file" menu

Justification can be specified in the form sheet or directly in the menu. As in MacWrite, there is also the possibility of using a ruler. Paragraphs typed directly after the formatted one, receive the same format, but they can be changed separately. The ¶ is used to tell where a paragraph ends (¶ can be shown or hidden). The ¶, one way or another, contains the formatting information of the preceding paragraph. One ¶ can be copied and pasted instead of another, whereby this paragraph gets the format of the former. A text with the ¶s visible is shown in Fig. A16.

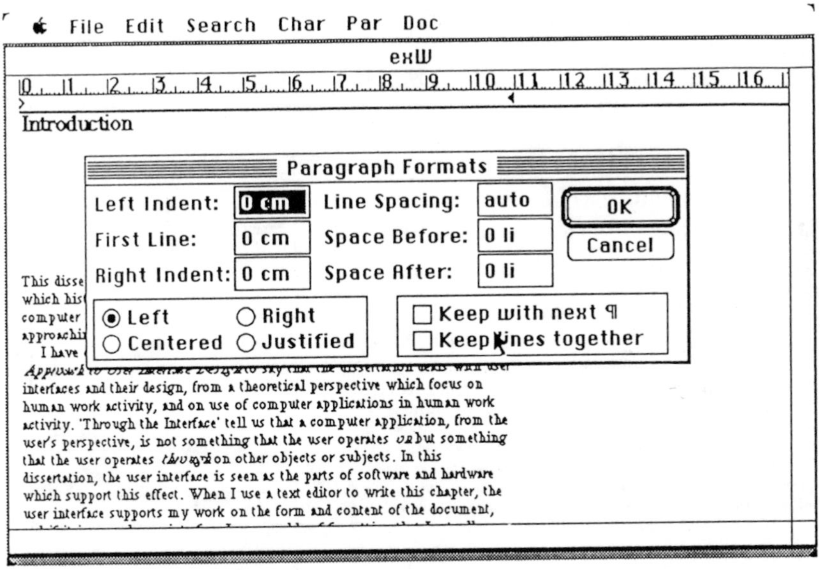

 File   Edit   Search   Char   Par   Doc

exW

|0, |1, |2, |3, |4, |5, |6, |7, |8, |9, |10 |11 |12 |13 |14 |15 |16 |

Introduction

Paragraph Formats

Left Indent:	0 cm	Line Spacing:	auto	OK
First Line:	0 cm	Space Before:	0 li	Cancel
Right Indent:	0 cm	Space After:	0 li	

⦿ Left   ◯ Right   ☐ Keep with next ¶
◯ Centered ◯ Justified   ☐ Keep lines together

This disse
which his
computer
approachi
I have

Approach to user interface design so say that the dissertation deals with user interfaces and their design, from a theoretical perspective which focus on human work activity, and on use of computer applications in human work activity. 'Through the Interface' tell us that a computer application, from the user's perspective, is not something that the user operates on but something that the user operates through on other objects or subjects. In this dissertation, the user interface is seen as the parts of software and hardware which support this effect. When I use a text editor to write this chapter, the user interface supports my work on the form and content of the document,

Fig. A13. The form sheet where formats for individual paragraphs can be changed (within the limits of the format of the document in general). Some of the parameters can be changed by typing into the boxes (the top half), other are toggles which can be changed by clicking the mouse in the boxes (the bottom half)

Font style can be changed directly in the pull-down menu, whereas fonts need to be changed via a sheet similar to the form sheet (Fig. A17 and 18). Font size can be changed in different ways, either by using this sheet or with different key-stroke combinations. The available font sizes are shown to the user, but scaling to any point size can be made (between 4 and 127 points). Headings and footings are created by typing a text, selecting it, and selecting the "running head" entry in the "Doc" menu (Fig. A19 shows this and Fig. A20 shows the effect). The heading must be placed in absolute figures contrary to the rest of the measures in WORD, which are placed in relation to the page margins. There is no way that one can see on the screen where the heading will be placed on paper. Automatic page numbering can be used.

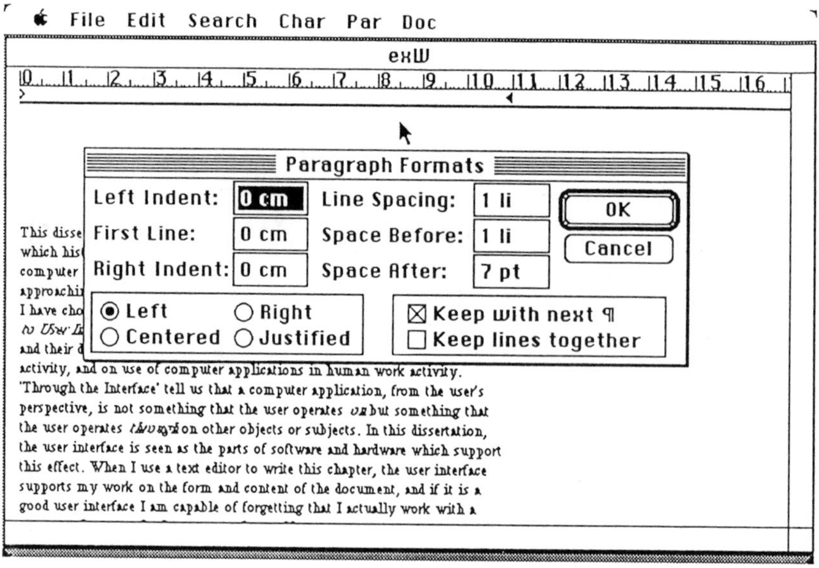

Fig. A14. Some of the parameters have been changed, including line spacing and extra leading

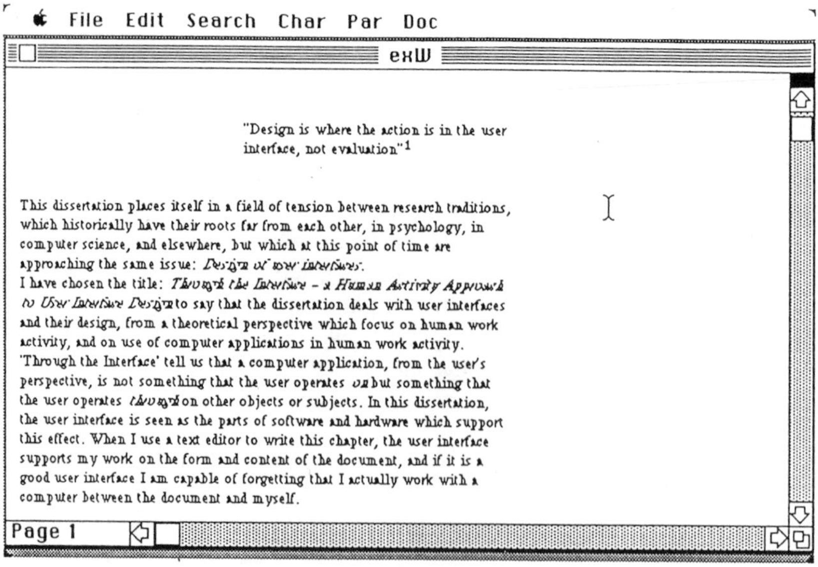

Fig. A15. The text after formatting using the parameters of Fig. A14

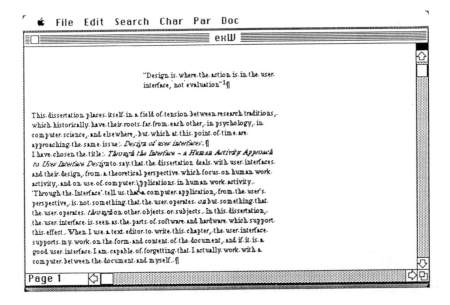

Fig. A16. Text with ¶s shown, indicating the end of each paragraph in the document. The ¶s are shown by issuing the "show ¶s" in the "Edit" menu

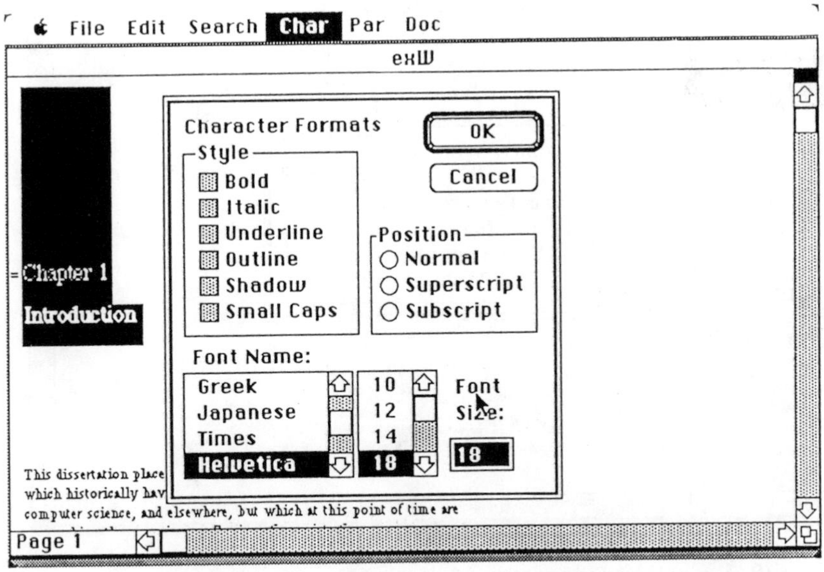

Fig. A17. The character sheet is used to change typography. Style and position is chosen via toggles, whereas the font and size is chosen by pointing, or, for the size, by typing

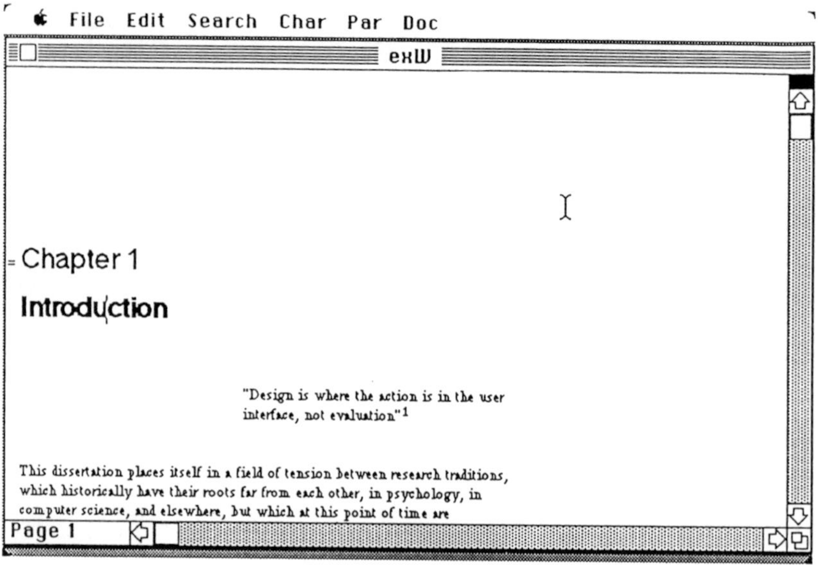

 File   Edit   Search   Char   Par   Doc

exW

= Chapter 1

Introduction

"Design is where the action is in the user
interface, not evaluation"[1]

This dissertation places itself in a field of tension between research traditions,
which historically have their roots far from each other, in psychology, in
computer science, and elsewhere, but which at this point of time are

Page 1

Fig. A18. The text changed according to the parameters of Fig. A17

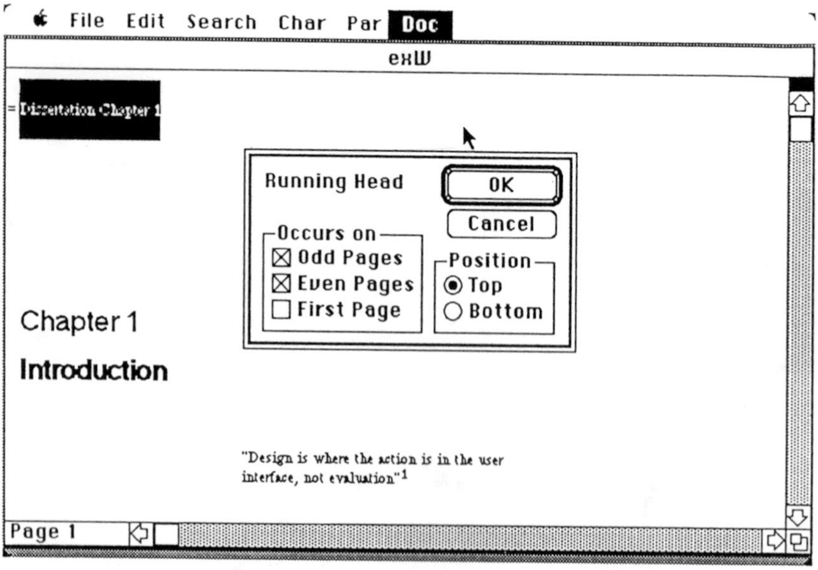

 File   Edit   Search   Char   Par   **Doc**

exW

= Dissertation Chapter 1

Running Head   [OK]

┌─Occurs on─   [Cancel]
⊠ Odd Pages   ┌─Position─
⊠ Even Pages   ⦿ Top
☐ First Page   ○ Bottom

Chapter 1

Introduction

"Design is where the action is in the user
interface, not evaluation"[1]

Page 1

*Fig. A19. A running head is created by typing a text for the heading,
selecting it, and choosing "running head" in the "Doc" menu. The menu
shows up by which the heading can be placed on the preferred pages*

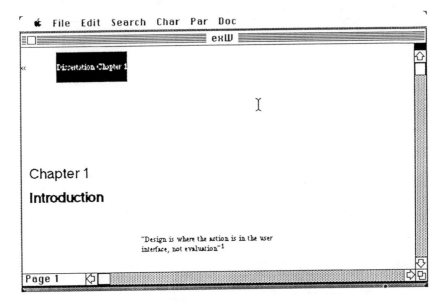

Fig. A20. The running head placed in the document according to the parameters of Fig. A19

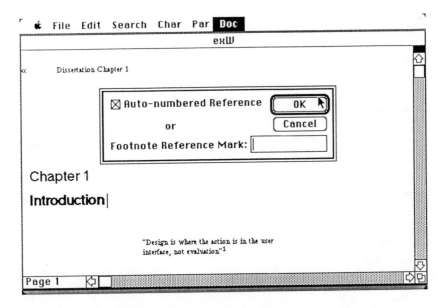

Fig. A21. Creating a footnote by choosing "footnote" in the "Doc" menu. The footnote will be inserted where the | is placed. The user can choose between automatic numbering of footnotes, and reference marks

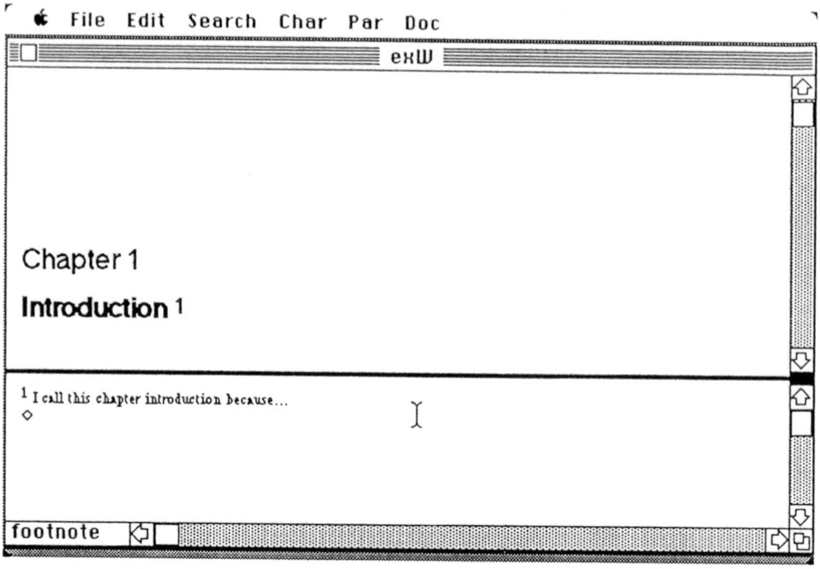

File Edit Search Char Par Doc

≡ eʜШ ≡

Chapter 1

Introduction [1]

---

[1] I call this chapter introduction because...

◇

footnote

Fig. A22. Typing the footnote text in the special footnote window at the bottom of the screen

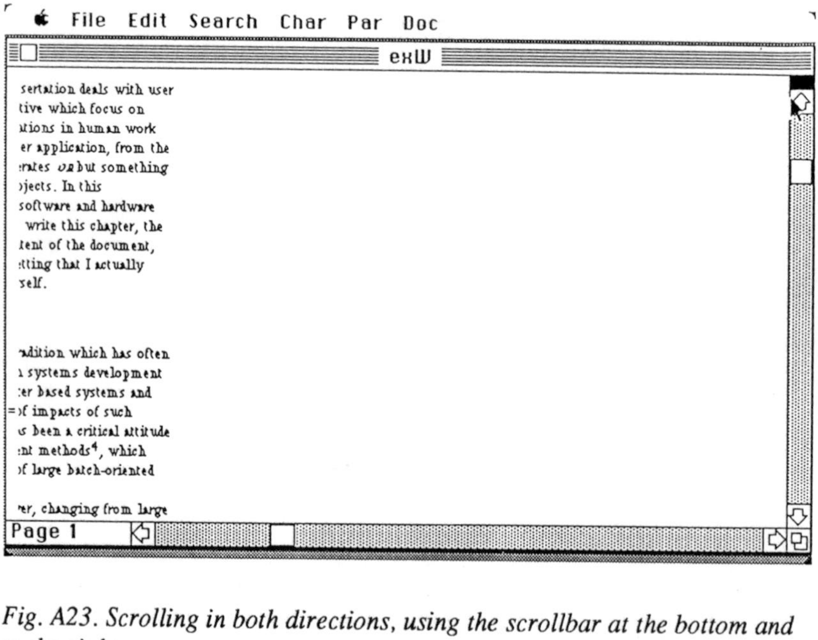

File Edit Search Char Par Doc

≡ eʜШ ≡

sertation deals with user
tive which focus on
ations in human work
er application, from the
erates or but something
)jects. In this
software and hardware
 write this chapter, the
tent of the document,
:tting that I actually
self.

ddition which has often
a systems development
:er based systems and
=)f impacts of such
is been a critical attitude
:nt methods[4], which
of large batch-oriented

*er, changing from large

Page 1

Fig. A23. Scrolling in both directions, using the scrollbar at the bottom and to the right

Footnotes can be created, and they are shown in a separate window. In general, the footnotes can be treated like the text, although there are some restrictions. By selecting "footnote" in the "Doc" menu, a footnote reference is placed in the text where the cursor is located. A prompt shows up to make the user choose between auto-numbered references or special reference marks (Fig. A21). After that, the footnote window opens (if it is not open already), and the footnote text can be entered (Fig. A22).

Scrolling can be done in both directions by means of the horizontal and vertical scrollbars (Fig. A23). The restrictions in work size are that one usually works with a small document, such as a scientific paper, not a report such as this book. This means that when one approaches 100 pages or 200 footnotes, response time becomes extremely long.

---

[1] MacWrite version number 4.5, dated April 4, 1985, the Danish version.

[2] Microsoft WORD version 1.05 dated April 24, 1985.

[3] Whereas I use a primarily English version of WORD in the examples, it has not been possible to get an English version of MacWrite, as this cannot be purchased in Denmark.

[4] The reader must excuse the lack of screen images with pull-down windows pulled down. Such images are impossible to make with the software presently available at the Department of Computer Science.

[5] See, for example, Sundblad, Y. (Ed.) (1987). *Quality and interaction in computer-aided graphic design* (UTOPIA Report No. 15). Stockholm: Arbetslivscentrum.

[6] Note the mixture of Danish and English text.